Our Feet into the Way of Peace

Holistic Approaches to Peace-building in the Context
of the Pilgrimage of Justice and Peace

Ibrahim Wushishi Yusuf
Jin Yang Kim (Editors)

OUR FEET INTO THE WAY OF PEACE
Ibrahim Wushishi Yusuf and Jin Yang Kim

© 2022 WCC Publications & Globethics.net
Globethics.net, Geneva.
Globethics.net PJP Series.
Director: Prof. Dr Obiora Ike, Executive Director of Globethics.net in
Geneva and Professor of Ethics at the Godfrey Okoye University Enugu/Nigeria.
Managing Editor: Dr Ignace Haaz, Globethics.net.

Coordinator Editor WCC Publications: Lyn van Rooyen
Cover and book design: Michael Cagnoni
Cover Photo Credit: Albin Hillert
Web ISBN 978-2-88931-474-4
Print ISBN 978-2-88931-475-1

World Council of Churches
150 route de Ferney, P.O. Box 2100
1211 Geneva 2, Switzerland
https://www.oikoumene.org
Email: publications@wcc-coe.org.

Globethics.net International
Secretariat
150 route de Ferney
1211 Geneva 2, Switzerland
https://www.globethics.net
Email: publications@globethics.net

CONTENTS

Introduction:

Why this Book—The Pilgrimage of Justice and Peace

Isabel Apawo Phiri

The World Council of Churches (WCC) assembly held in Busan in 2013 called on churches everywhere to walk together, to view their common life, their journey of faith, as a part of the Pilgrimage of Justice and Peace, and to join others in celebrating life and in taking concrete steps toward transforming injustices and violence. The invitation was to the WCC member churches, other Christians, people of other faiths, and people of good will to walk, work, and pray together. The WCC central committee meeting of July 2014 further clarified the pilgrimage. In *An Invitation to the Pilgrimage of Justice and Peace, they said:* "Declaring 'We intend to move together' and inviting all people of good will to 'join in pilgrimage,' the delegates of the Busan assembly responded in a new way to the contemporary contextual challenges for the witness and very being of the churches, to the needs of people and creation yearning for justice and peace, and to the perceptions of many young people eager to see signs of hope."

Through this document, it became clear that being on a Pilgrimage of Justice and Peace is participating in God's mission toward life; moving to issues and places relevant for life and survival of people and the earth; deepening the fellowship of churches on the way with a strong spiritual dimension of common prayer and theological reflection; participating in a journey of hope, looking for and celebrating signs of God's reign of justice and peace already here and now; and discovering opportunities for common witness and transformative action that make a difference in today's world with an open invitation to all people of good will.

In its invitation, the WCC central committee also noted that "the pilgrimage might consist of at least three different dimensions—not in a linear but much more in a dynamic, interdependent understanding": "Celebrating the Gifts *(via positiva),*" "Visiting the Wounds *(via negativa),*" and "Transforming the Injustices *(via transformativa).*" The committee recommended that "as a seven-year programme emphasis, the pilgrimage of justice and peace will combine community-based initiatives and national and international advocacy for Just Peace, focusing on life-affirming economies; climate change; nonviolent peacebuilding and reconciliation; and human dignity." It was expected that as the different regions and churches engaged with the themes, they would do so within their context, raising issues that were pertinent to them.

In 2015, the executive committee resolved that there should be annual foci of regions and themes as milestones and expressions of unity on the Pilgrimage of Justice and Peace. Since then, the following have been the focus themes and regions:

2015—Climate Justice and the United Nations Framework Convention on Climate Change (UNFCCC) COP21 in France/Europe. The Reference Group of the Pilgrimage of Justice and Peace had its first meeting at the Bossey Institute, Switzerland.

2016—Peacebuilding in the context of religion and violence. Syria, Iraq, and Israel and Palestine were the priority countries, and the region was Middle East. The Reference Group of the Pilgrimage of Justice and Peace had its second meeting in Jerusalem, Israel, and Palestine.

2017—Peacebuilding in the context of religion and violence. Nigeria, South Sudan, Democratic Republic of Congo, and Burundi were the priority countries, and the region was Africa. The Reference Group of the Pilgrimage of Justice and Peace had its third meeting in Abuja and Kaduna, Nigeria.

2018—Ecumenical Diakonia and Sustainable Development. This pilgrimage brought together WCC and ACT Alliance work on diakonia and development. Colombia was the priority country, and the region was Latin America and the Caribbean. The Reference Group of the Pilgrimage of Justice and Peace had its fourth meeting in Bogota, Colombia. This was the third meeting of the Theological Study Group and the first joint meeting of the Reference Group of the Pilgrimage of Justice and Peace and the Theological Study Group. For the first time, the members of the Reference Group went on Pilgrim Team Visits (PTVs) before the joint meeting. One PTV went to Apartadó, Curaradó, and Chocó, in Colombia. The second PTV went to Cali and Cauca, Colombia. The third PTV went to Valledupar, Barranquilla, and Cartagena, Colombia. They focused on issues related to the peace process, gender-based violence, land-based injustices, racism, and displacement. This experience shaped the joint meeting, and it was decided that in future meetings, the Theological Study Group should also be part of the PTVs.

2019—Racism. The region was Asia. The general secretary of the Christian Conference of Asia and general secretaries of some National Council of Churches in Asia requested that racism in Asia be analyzed through the lens of "Building Peace and Human Dignity." PTVs took place from 28 February to 2 March. As agreed in 2018 the Theological Study Group joined the PTV. Visits took place in the following countries: Myanmar, the border between Thailand and Myanmar, Bangladesh, India, and Pakistan. The PTVs were followed by a joint meeting of the Reference Group and the Theological Study Group, in which the members reflected on the context of Asia through the lens of racism.

The practice of Pilgrim Team Visits was a methodology to show solidarity. Through analysis of the PTVs by the Reference Group and the Theological Study Group, related themes began to emerge. The lived experiences of the people visited were summarized in four themes: truth and trauma, land and development, gender justice, and racial justice.

This publication is a reflection on the lived experiences of the pilgrimage from the perspective of people from Burundi, the Democratic Republic of Congo, Nigeria, the Korean Peninsula, Palestine and Israel, South Sudan, Syria, Ukraine, and Colombia.

Bernard Ntahoturi highlights the timely solidarity visit led by the WCC leadership in 2016, which prompted churches to develop a strategic plan of action for peace and reconciliation in Burundi. The harvest workshop on the Pilgrimage of Justice and Peace, which took place in Burundi in 2020, helped the churches in Burundi to renew their commitment to promoting sustainable peace and economic development.

Paul Mpongo Tshihamba shows that the Pilgrimage of Justice and Peace has been the strategic tool for the churches in the Democratic Republic of Congo (DRC) to promote justice and peace. He emphasizes the ecumenical cooperation of churches in the DRC with churches around the world, in civil society, and in the Catholic church.

Celine Osukwu discusses the role of religious institutions in the peacebuilding process. She describes the WCC's women's pilgrimage, "Walking Her Story," as a solidarity journey reminding churches and agencies to vigorously pursue the course of justice and peace, especially for women, children, persons with disabilities, and all others who bear the brunt of conflicts.

Ephraim Yakubu Simon also highlights the "Walking Her Story" pilgrimage, along with the visit of the WCC leadership in 2016, as landmarks in the peacebuilding process in Nigeria. These initiatives have strengthened ecumenical bonds and interfaith collaboration in our efforts to build peace.

Emanuel Youkhana underlines many initiatives of the Iraqi churches in the peacebuilding process, including the Iraqi churches' invitation of Pope Francis to Iraq in 2021. This was a historic step in the path of peaceful coexistence between Iraqi ethno-religious and cultural components.

Seung-min Shin notes many initiatives by the Korean churches for peace and reunification on the Korean Peninsula since the WCC 10th assembly in Busan, including the Demilitarized Zone/DMZ Human Chain Movement, organized by churches and civil society in Korea; a pilgrimage of young people to the DMZ in 2019; a peace convocation, coordinated by the Presbyterian Church in the Republic of Korea; and the Global Prayer Campaign in 2020. He states that a key lesson from these peacebuilding experiences is that we should solidify the international bonds in this journey.

In the case of Israel and Palestine, **Munib A. Younan** reminds the reader about the call of the churches in Palestine to the ecumenical movement to come and see the suffering of the Palestinians under Israeli occupation. The Ecumenical Accompaniment Program in Palestine and Israel has been accompanying local people and communities, offering a protective presence, and witnessing their daily struggles and hopes.

James Oyet Latansio gives insights into the complex situation of the people in South Sudan who are impacted by trauma. The churches' firm commitment to peacebuilding is an integral part of the healing process.

Michel Nseir uses his 10-year work experience with Syria to provide insight on what it means to contribute toward peacebuilding there. He discusses the churches' initiatives and efforts toward peace, which included the international ecumenical conference on Christian presence and witness in the Middle East in 2013 and the WCC consultation on the crisis in Syria in 2019.

In the last article on "The World Council of Churches' engagement for Just Peace in Colombia," **Marcelo Schneider** analyses how the WCC started this work, the difficulties encountered in duplicating the Ecumenical Accompaniment Programme in Palestine and Israel in Colombia, and how the work continued through the various peace-building initiatives of the local churches in Colombia. He shows that church ownership of peace-building programmes is essential before international ecumenical bodies' participation. He also highlighted that the interest of WCC leadership in peace-building in Colombia has been essential because it opened the door to engage the political leadership on both sides of the political divide. The use of the Pilgrim Team Visits methodology allowed the WCC to capture the concerns of the people on the margins of the society in Colombia.

Since 24 February 2022, when Russia invaded Ukraine, there have been several attempts by governments and faith communities to promote a ceasefire. The WCC has issued statements and, with ACT Alliance, sent a delegation to visit refugee centres and church-based organizations providing humanitarian responses within Ukraine and in neighbouring countries.

The WCC also convened two **ecumenical round tables** on the situation in Ukraine in March and June 2022. This publication includes the messages resulting from that those consultations.

Prof. Dr Isabel Apawo Phiri
Deputy general secretary of the World Council of Churches.

1

Overview of the Peacebuilding Process in Burundi

Bernard Ntahoturi

In analyzing the work of peace and reconciliation in Burundi, we should start by understanding the nature of the conflict there and in the wider Great Lakes region of Africa. Some view it as an ethnic problem, a political issue; others see it as a socio-economic problem. It is generally agreed that the root causes of the conflict go back to the colonial manipulations which led to ethnic crystallization, together with the mismanagement of the post-colonial era by the Burundi elite, which brought with it violence and authoritarianism. Many studies on the Burundi crises (1965, 1969, 1972, 1988, and 1993) have shown that the deterioration of socio-cultural values and the struggle around power management aggravated an already fragile situation.

Explorers, missionaries, and colonizers who later visited Burundi and governed the region classified the Burundi population as races, tribes, or ethnic groups The first sign of ethnic cleavage appeared during the establishment of the Belgian policy of indirect rule in 1930s. From the time of independence in 1962 and the abolition of the monarchy, the main problem was gaining access to power, then maintaining and exercising it. Since 1962, Burundi has been marked by a succession of violent social political crises that have disrupted its national cohesion and compromised its economic and social development. Bad governance characterized by a political and social exclusion system has led to political and ethnic clashes. There has been a struggle for power and influence, especially between the Hutu and the Tutsi. During this time, the population experienced poverty, injustice, sickness, exploitation, lack of dialogue, divisions of all kinds, intolerance, violence, and even war. This culminated in the Arusha negotiations that gave a framework for the Burundi Peace and Reconciliation Agreement in 2000, bringing to an end a thirteen-year war.

In this context, the National Council of Churches of Burundi developed its ministry of peacebuilding. The churches have been involved for struggle for justice and peace throughout the years. The WCC invitation to join in the Pilgrimage of Justice and Peace and the identification of Burundi as one of the priority countries in the pilgrimage has strengthened the long struggle of the churches in the peace process.

The solidarity visit led by the former WCC general secretary, Rev. Dr Olav Fykse Tveit, affirmed the commitment of the fellowship to accompany the peace process in Burundi. One of the main outcomes of that visit was the development of a Strategic Plan of Action for Peace and Reconciliation (SAPPR). Since then, the SAPPR has become a foundation for engagement and advocacy documents for the churches locally and internationally. Since the Busan assembly, Burundi has welcomed the Pilgrim Team Visit in 2016 and the women's harvest workshop in 2020. We have continued to maintain the spirit of resilience as churches in the face of all challenges, with hope that peace, stability, and economic development will be achieved for all through our collective efforts.

Reflection on the Burundi Churches' Engagement in the Peacebuilding Process

Since its creation, the Burundi National Council of Churches (CNEB), with the help of its partners, has been active in the process of peacebuilding. This was made possible with the help of its ecumenical and international partners. This work of peacebuilding was especially intensified after the WCC assembly in Busan and the ecumenical visits in Burundi, namely the WCC Pilgrimage Team Visit in 2017 and the Pilgrimage of Justice and Peace experience harvesting Workshop in 2020. Faithful to the command of Jesus Christ, church members are tireless in proclaiming the good news, and offering the prospect of social reconciliation through extended pastoral services. The CNEB has been a good listener to the many brothers and sisters who are asking for help and compassion, as in the parable of the good Samaritan (Luke 10:29–37). Responding to Jesus' call to his followers in Matthew 25:31–46, the CNEB offers aid to many people who are poor and in need of human warmth, giving witness to God's love. Other efforts have been concentrated in the areas described below.

Church participation in the May 2020 elections

Prior to the May 2020 general elections, there were tensions between political parties and sporadic confrontations in the provinces of the countries. The population was afraid amidst this tension, as has been the case every time the country organizes elections. We as Christian church leaders, together with the interfaith community, came together and discussed the situation and the ways in which we could contribute to the stability of the country before, during, and after the elections. We then discussed the situation with the presidents of the registered political parties in the country. We strongly urged the political parties to make sure their members respected the rights of the population to exercise their right to vote according to their conscience.

Furthermore, the church, through the CNEB, in collaboration with other faith groups, was able to mobilize the religious community to actively participate in the general elections. We reminded the Burundi people of the need to respect human life, remembering that they would continue to live together after the elections. We organized activities on civic education, and we mobilized, trained, and deployed election observers from the religious communities for the different regions. This was our contribution to free, fair, credible, and peaceful elections in Burundi, and I think, it contributed greatly to changing the narrative of the Burundi elections. For the first time, elections were considered to be free and peaceful. I see this as a big gift from the church to the people of Burundi in our journey for a just peace.

Gender justice and peace

In our engagement as churches in the Pilgrimage of Justice and Peace in Burundi, we discovered the negative impacts of gender-based violence (GBV) on women and girls from different regions, from the higher to the lowest levels. Although women continue to represent the highest percentage of victims, there has been an increase in male victims. At the end of 2020, the data collected in the field-based services of the Ministry of National Solidarity, Social Affairs, Human Rights and Gender revealed that 15,307 people were victims of sexual and gender-based violence (SGBV). Among them, 12,663 victims were women, and 2644 were men (82.7 and 17.3 per cent, respectively). The reflections and experiences shared during the women's harvest Pilgrimage of Justice and Peace workshop held in March 2020 confirmed these challenges. The COVID-19 pandemic lockdown aggravated the situation in Burundi.

The government of Burundi has different programmes to combat the menace of SBGV. However, as a faith community, we realized that the victims are our church members and that the voice of the church is needed in order to help eradicate GBV and seek justice for the victims. Therefore, the churches, through the CNEB, convened a consultation of church leaders on the theme of "Faith actors at the forefront of the fight against GBV: transforming social norms to promote gender justice." Participants in the consultation were drawn from the government ministry, church leaders, women, youth, and civil societies to reflect on this challenge and how to respond to it. Some of the activities during the consultations included reflections on the root causes of GBV and how church leaders can be agents of change. There were biblical reflections addressing issues of gender-based violence. The biblical reflections opened the minds of the participants as to how God is a God of justice and how there is a need for churches to strengthen activities aimed at combatting GBV. The use of the media has been identified as an important tool in addressing this menace. The response to GBV is an important component of the pilgrimage of justice and peace among the churches in Burundi. It has given us the opportunity to provide pastoral and psychosocial accompaniment for and with the victims even in the face of COVID-19 lockdown.

Prospects for the Future

In many countries in Africa, the church is the only institution that functions well., It enables people to continue to live and hope for a better future. Developments that have taken place during the last 20 years offer new challenges and opportunities for the church's mission in Burundi. Therefore, going forward, the church should continue to promote the positive values within the Burundi culture in the following ways:

- The love of joint effort. The Burundi people attach great importance to labour as a source of livelihood and prosperity. The church should underscore this value as a way of promoting peace and economic empowerment.

- The value of *ubushingantahe*. This term describes a culture of truth, a sense of justice, a sense of family and social responsibility, faithfulness in keeping promises, peaceful resolution of conflicts through conciliation, arbitration, and mediation, dialogue and collaboration, and a spirit of understanding and reconciliation.

- Moral values of social harmony, honour, respect for human dignity, sacredness of human life, communal living *(ubuntu)*, and the like.

- Sense of probity; that is to say, justice for all, truth and honesty, respect for life, and equal dignity.

These values must be at the centre of our pilgrimage.

Conclusion

The church's purpose in the world is to make visible the presence of God in time and space. It is to open the world to God's grace and love for all. We as a church must consistently remind ourselves of Jesus' proclamation to his followers (Matt. 5:13–16): we are the salt of the world; we are the light of the world.

Réflexion sur l'engagement œcuménique des Églises de République démocratique du Congo (RDC) en faveur de la consolidation de la justice, de la paix et de la sécurité en RDC

Paul MPONGO Tshihamba

Contexte général

Il importe de rappeler dans quel contexte la RDC a été retenue comme pays prioritaire à côté des autres. Celui-ci s'est caractérisé par des crises multiformes, dues aux ratés des élections présidentielles et législatives de 2006, 2011 et 2018, qui se sont soldées par les guerres des minerais à l'est de la RDC, ainsi que par du braconnage et par le pillage des ressources naturelles. Le COE a décidé d'accompagner les Églises de RDC dans leurs efforts pour consolider la justice, la paix et la sécurité dans leur pays au titre du programme du Pèlerinage de justice et de paix.

Les actions concrètes des Églises de RDC dans la consolidation de la justice et de la paix

Sur le plan œcuménique, les Églises membres du COE en RDC collaborent avec la société civile, l'Église catholique et l'Église du Christ au Congo. Elles se sont mobilisées pour consolider la justice et la paix en organisant des marches de protestation, en menant des plaidoyers, en rédigeant des déclarations politiques, et en proposant des cadres de réflexion et de renforcement des capacités par le biais de séminaires, de colloques, des symposiums ou d'ateliers de réflexion sur des sujets de société variés:

- des questions d'actualité choquantes (viols, violences, violations de divers droits),

- la bonne gouvernance, la lutte contre la corruption et le chômage,

- la protection de l'environnement, le réchauffement climatique, la réduction de la production de gaz à effet de serre,

- les violences basées sur le genre, l'autonomisation des femmes

- l'encadrement des jeunes en matière d'entrepreneuriat, le renforcement des capacités pour faciliter la prise d'autonomie, la réinsertion sociale,

- l'encouragement des personnes à mobilité réduite pour une véritable transformation sociale.

Outre leurs activités d'éducation civique et de changement de mentalités, elles ont mené plusieurs formations en lien avec les élections:

- formation des observateurs et observatrices et des témoins,

- formation à la gestion ou à la transformation pacifiques des conflits avant, pendant et après les élections.

L'accompagnement du COE auprès des Églises membres de la RDC

Après Busan en 2013, le COE a concrètement accompagné les Églises de la RDC dans le cadre du Pèlerinage de justice et de paix, les aidant à consolider la justice, la paix et la sécurité à travers plusieurs initiatives: supports, visites, encouragements et prières pour le peuple de RDC, plaidoyer auprès de l'ONU et visioconférences à destination du peuple congolais.

En 2015, une délégation de haut niveau du COE s'est rendue en RDC pour s'enquérir de la situation sur le terrain, sous la conduite du secrétaire général d'alors, le pasteur Olav Fykse Tveit. Il était accompagné de Peter Prove, du père Buda et de Mme Segma. Le COE a ensuite convoqué un forum sur la sécurité et la paix en RDC, auquel 25 personnes ont été conviées. Malheureusement, l'ambassade suisse à Kinshasa n'a pu délivrer que huit visas. Les recommandations de Genève ont abouti à un programme de suivi pour aider les Églises à bâtir la justice et la paix à travers des actions de sensibilisation et de renforcement des capacités. Le pasteur Tveit et la délégation de haut niveau étaient aussi à Kinshasa pour parler avec les responsables politiques et les candidats malheureux aux élections présidentielles. Ils ont bénéficié de l'appui de l'ONU en RDC et leur travail a permis d'apaiser ces conflits et de consolider l'amour et la tolérance entre les protagonistes. Le COE est encore présent aujourd'hui, offrant son assistance financière par le biais de structures permanentes telles que le programme EHAIA, dirigé par Isis Kangudia depuis la mort d'Andrew Lusey, ou encore le programme d'appui aux personnes à mobilité réduite, dans le cadre du master en transformation sociale que dirigeait la défunte Micheline Kamba, paix à son âme.

En 2017-2018, sous la direction de M. Nigussu Legesse, le COE a financé la formation des témoins et observateurs ou observatrices pour les élections. L'Église du Christ au Congo a contribué à cette activité avec les Églises membres du COE, mais ces dernières n'ont pas été associées à la gestion de l'aide financière.

En 2021, accompagnés par le pasteur Wushishi Ibrahim Yusuf, les Églises membres du COE et le programme EHAIA ont obtenu un soutien financier pour organiser des activités dans le cadre du PJP, dans le but de dénoncer les injustices, les violences basées sur le genre, les abus du pouvoir, de mettre fin à la corruption et de plaider en faveur de la bonne gouvernance et de l'état de droit. À la fin de ces activités, les chefs religieux des Églises membres ont signé une déclaration politique en forme de plaidoyer qui a été envoyée au président de la RDC, à l'ONU et au COE, et lue sur les antennes de la radio et de la télévision nationale.

Perspectives d'avenir après l'Assemblée de 2022 en Allemagne

La RDC compte sur le COE pour continuer à accompagner les Églises membres dans leurs efforts pour assurer une paix durable.

Des élections présidentielles et législatives sont prévues en 2023. L'Église a pour grande mission de former les observateurs et observatrices et les témoins des élections. Elle œuvre dans les domaines de l'éducation civique, de la formation au règlement pacifique des conflits, de la gestion des pandémies et du renforcement des capacités en vue de l'autonomisation des jeunes, des femmes et des personnes à mobilité réduite.

Rendons gloire à Dieu pour tout ce que nous avons pu réaliser ensemble pendant ce pèlerinage.

Longue vie au COE et à ses Églises membres à travers le monde, dans la nouvelle marche qui les attend.

Avec Dieu, nous accomplirons des exploits.

3

Churches' Ecumenical Engagement in Peacebuilding in Nigeria

Celine Osukwu

Introduction and Background to Conflicts in Nigeria

Nigeria, one of the largest countries in Africa, is multi-religious and multi-ethnic. The varied people and groups that make up Nigeria enjoyed a relatively peaceful coexistence until 2000 when the country started experiencing inter-ethnic and interreligious clashes. Prior to these clashes, other issues that endangered lives included poverty, inequality, injustice, corruption, human rights abuses, and unemployment. Suddenly, intolerance based on ethnic and religious differences, as well as squabbles between herders and farmers, ignited violence that increased in frequency and magnitude, especially in the northern part of Nigeria. The trend resulted in polarization, segregation, and wanton destruction.

In 2009, there was an uprising of the Islamic militants known as Boko Haram. Initially, Boko Haram seemed mainly to target Christians and churches as well as security agencies, but as time went on, the group attacked many others, including women, girls, and schoolchildren. In 2012, this led to Nigeria being identified as the country where the most severe violence between Christians and Muslims was taking place, second only to the Bosnian experience of 1993–95. Young men were forcefully conscripted; thousands of people were kidnapped, and many more people were subjected to forced labour, as well as physical and psychological torture. From 2014 until approximately 2019, over 6600 people were killed. Over 3 million people were displaced. Resources and farms were destroyed, leading to severe food insecurity. Thousands of women and children (including the 276 Chibok school girls) were abducted, held captive, raped, and/or forced into marriage. Many of the girls have given birth to children from repeated rapes. When those abducted return home from captivity, they are rejected, marginalized, and stigmatized by their friends, family, and communities. The ordeal of these most vulnerable groups, who bear the heaviest brunt of the attacks and conflicts, is not yet over.

Overview of Peacebuilding Process

Building peace in conflict-prone zones is a long-term process that involves prevention of conflict, managing conflict, resolving conflict or transformation of conflict, and post-conflict reconciliation or trauma healing.

Military confrontation

In Nigeria, a country bedevilled by numerous clashes raging over two decades, the government initially adopted a strategy of military confrontation and later formed a joint task force with neighbouring countries to manage the conflict. Though all villages and towns taken by the militants were liberated and people were encouraged to return to their original homes, the military confrontations did not yield lasting peace. Military confrontation is widely perceived as having fallen short in protecting human interests or enhancing human agency. This approach lacks provision for humanitarian aid. It does not create opportunities or empowerment for affected but weak groups to talk. It also fails to improve the moral-political climate.

State peace institutions

Recently, the governments of Kaduna, Plateau, and Adamawa—states in the middle belt that are most affected by the conflict—have established peace institutions with initiatives capable of curbing ethnic, religious, and farmer-herder conflicts. Unfortunately, so far, the new institutions are facing discouraging funding and structural issues.

Activities of religious institutions

Religious institutions play instrumental roles in the peacebuilding process. Religion is directly or indirectly implicated in many conflicts. Because of this, Indigenous religious groups can play significant roles in providing spiritual, emotional, and psychological support to those who have suffered attacks. There has been an increased number of religiously based citizen groups focused on bringing about peace, justice, and reconciliation.

As major stakeholders, religious institutions have sponsored interreligious peace conferences, such as those organized by the Christian Council of Nigeria (CAN), with Muslim groups, traditional leaders, and government officials. Another was held by members of the Christian Reformed Church in North America for 54 religious leaders drawn from the local Reformed churches, CAN, traditional chiefs, politicians, and local government officials.

In 2013, the World Council of Churches (WCC), representing churches around the world, led an international delegation of Christians and Muslims—who were represented by the Royal Jordanian Aal Al-Bayt Institute of Islamic Thought—in a fact-finding visit to search for common ground. The report of the visit was widely circulated, and it formed the basis for further engagement by both state and non-state actors. The WCC has partnered with other faith-based organizations in follow-up visits. Interviews, as well as a women's Pilgrim Team Visit, have reminded churches and agencies to vigorously pursue the course of justice and peace, especially for the women, children, persons with disabilities, and all others who bear the brunt of conflicts.

Peace education

Non-religious peacebuilding groups have intensified their efforts to educate and train people in peacebuilding and conflict resolution. Most of these NGOs target religious groups as ripe for training and mobilization. In the same way, faith-based relief and development NGOs have expanded their mandates and training to include peacebuilding activities. Religious actors who have served as educators are also incorporating peace education into their educational activities. Nowadays, many faith-based NGOs support peace education programs that include specific training in conflict resolution, democracy, or human rights. Some are also developing peace curricula for schools or training educators on issues such as justice and reconciliation.

Churches' Engagement in the Peacebuilding Process

Churches in Nigeria, alongside ecumenical partners around the world, affirm that sustaining and protecting lives is at the centre of the Christian calling. Because religion is fundamental to individual and social conceptions of peace, churches have been actively involved in activities that aim at resolving injustice in nonviolent ways. The 16-member Christian Council of Nigeria (CCN) carried out several peace campaign activities, issuing statements and paying visits to religious leaders and government officials. Churches also engaged in interreligious dialogue with Islamic leaders and organizations such as the Supreme Council for Islamic Affairs (SCIA) and the Jama'tul Nasril Islam (JNI), both led by His Eminence the Sultan of Sokoto.

As the interreligious conflicts became more frequent, the CCN joined forces with the Christian Association of Nigeria (CAN) and some Muslim counterparts in a bid to find the best ways to resolve issues. The efforts of the CCN to foster dialogue between Christians and Muslims caught the attention of the German Embassy in Nigeria, and the leadership of the CCN was invited to visit Germany in 2013, along with the Sultan of Sokoto and other prominent leaders of the Muslim community in Nigeria, and the Catholic Archbishop of Abuja. This engagement strengthened the conviction of the ecumenical body that mainstreaming peacebuilding in its programming has become imperative. Churches also form interreligious peacebuilding organizations with Muslim and Traditional religious groups. They engage in training programs to educate religious leaders on issues relevant to peacebuilding work.

Churches have been offering healing and reintegration programs that play aid in the broader psycho-social recovery of individuals and communities. Many churches have helped to provide emotional and spiritual support to conflict-affected communities. CCN and some churches have developed trauma healing programs. Many, like the Bishara Baptist Church in Idi-Araba Lagos and St Theresa's Catholic Church in Yola, have served victims and survivors as emergency homes. St Theresa's Church has housed more than 500 internally displaced persons, most of whom are women and children. Churches thus provide elements of the resources needed for the rebuilding process.

Churches have also incorporated peacebuilding activities into their outreach and development work. In 2013, the Christian Council of Churches adopted a resolution during its 28th General Assembly held in Uyo, Akwa Ibom State, to dedicate its Institute of Church and Society (ICS), located in northern Nigeria, to the work of promoting peace in Nigeria. ICS is currently housing a peace-building and trauma-healing project through which Christian and Islamic leaders, as well as Traditional religious leaders from 19 states in northern Nigeria, receive training on peacebuilding and conflict management. Trauma healing is one of the peacebuilding processes engaged in by the churches.

As a member of the WCC, the CCN shares in the commitment to interreligious peace and social justice and has been involved in many local and international peace initiatives since 2013. In 2016, following the 2013 fact-finding visit of the international delegation of Muslim and Christian leaders led by the WCC and the Royal Jordanian Aal Al-Bayt Institute of Islamic Thought, the International Centre for Interfaith, Peace and Harmony (ICIPH) was established. The Centre remains a joint project encouraging peaceful co-existence of all factions.

Pilgrim Team Visit to Nigeria

The 2017 Pilgrim Team Visit to Nigeria, known as "Walking Her Story," was not only a response to the call to churches everywhere to walk together and to view their common life as part of the Pilgrimage of Justice and Peace. It was also a process of sustaining life-affirming solidarity and action. Though the UN recognized that women play vital roles in securing the three pillars of sustainable peace, the prevailing patriarchal culture of Nigerian societies hardly recognizes the salient roles of women. In Nigeria's context of instability and conflict, women—victims and survivors of all sorts of horrendous treatments—are bottled up with many stories of pain, triumph, and victory. So the pilgrims went on a mission of harnessing these unheard and unshared stories to serve as therapeutic frameworks for learning. The team's objectives were to listen to the stories of women's experiences, agency, resilience, and success; to identify practices that have been developed for achieving just peace; to discern and analyze the roles of women religious leaders in transforming structures and practices and issues of injustice and violence, and to document and share stories with the wider ecumenical movement.

A storytelling approach was adopted, and the team was guided by the biblically based notion of "living letters": listening and learning about the role of women and how culture and religion may intersect in the expression of Christian compassion in contexts of violence. Pilgrims were also guided by the goals of solidarity and accompaniment. Within the motif of care, the pilgrims listened and interrogated the role of religion and culture to understand the realities of gender injustice and the conflicts caused by religion. Broad-based consultative approaches with stakeholders—interactive and debriefing sessions—were applied. The team analyzed the stories shared, which enabled an understanding of the depths of pain, hurt, and guilt experienced.

In Abuja, the team visited and interacted with representatives of agencies that have a stake in the well-being of Nigeria. These include the Catholic Archbishop of Abuja, the president of the Christian Association of Nigeria, the executive secretary of Abuja National Mosque Management, the UN Women Office, and the Country Representative UN High Commissioner for Refugees. The team worshipped at EYN, the Church of the Brethren, Nigeria—one of the churches that suffer the most from Boko Haram's heinous activities. Although Brethren churches elsewhere do so, EYN is one of the churches that have yet to ordain women, although a lot of women members are trained theologians. The team also met some women who narrated their stories of horrendous experiences in the northern part of Nigeria.

In Jos, Plateau State, pilgrims had interactive sessions with religious leaders, peace practitioners, media, civil society activists, security agencies, and relevant government departments. Issues raised included access to land rights and resources, health care, protection and trauma healing, influence of faith and religion on conflicts, sexual and gender-based violence, and women's roles and participation in leadership.

Pilgrims visited the Paramount Traditional ruler, the Gbong Gwon Jos, His Majesty, Da Gyang Buba. He said, "The biggest confusion is globalization, which is leading to a gradual disappearance of communities from their communal living. . . . I am because you are. . . . The day we realize that we are created for relationship, the peace will come. . . . Christ warned us to keep prepared. If we can learn to prepare, there will be peace. . . . We should avoid judging each other but allow the beauty of godliness be seen in us by the next person."

The team visited Riyom Internally Displaced Persons (IDP) Camp, about 47 km from Jos, one of the camps abandoned by both Nigerian government and humanitarian agencies. Riyom IDP Camp is a self-organized camp where displaced persons find refuge in abandoned buildings very close to the local government secretariat but without official management, assistance, or attention. Individuals in this unaccounted-for camp are supported only by NGOs. It hosts 500 people. Women and children constitute 75% of the inhabitants.

Pilgrims were at the Centre for Caring, Empowerment and Peace Initiative (CCEPI). The centre was founded by Dr Rebecca Dali. At the centre, we listened to touching stories of women beneficiaries of CCEPI intervention who were all direct victims of Boko Haram. Those were stories of pain, sorrow, and resilience. The storytellers ranged from widows whose husband soldiers were killed to orphans and women abducted and sold and resold by Boko Haram.

Pilgrims paid a visit to the Deputy Governor of Plateau State. Our spokesperson thanked the government and the people of the state for their hospitality and commended the government for establishing a peacebuilding agency and for the various projects that will bring about economic and socio-political transformation in the state.

In Adamawa State, the pilgrims met with 100 top Christian and Muslim religious leaders. The Christian Association of Nigeria and Muslim Council, the Women's Wing of CAN, and the Federation of Muslim Women Associations of Nigeria were platforms used to mobilize participants. The following issues came up: some politicians capitalize on the raging conflicts to divide people along religious lines; a divisive narrative exists among women and youth; there are religiously mixed families in the state that can inspire people to tolerate one another. Examples were stated of gender-based violence in the state. We heard inspiring stories, which included a Muslim providing water for the construction of a church auditorium and consultations on actions that may lead to an exchange of gifts during festive periods. Participants were encouraged to engage in joint projects like building schools for both Muslim and Christian children. Leaders were encouraged to refrain from hate speech and to use pulpits and minbars to preach peace, tolerance, and respect for human life and dignity.

The pilgrims visited the IDP camp at Fufore, which is one of the biggest camps in northeast Nigeria. Fufore is about 28 km away from Yola, the capital of Adamawa State. Fufore hosts over 1500 displaced persons. Pilgrims also visited St. Theresa's camp, a facility of the Catholic Diocese of Yola, housing over 500 displaced persons. This camp looked much better than all the other camps we visited. All children in the camp have clothes and are regularly fed. Most of the residents are women and children. In all the camps, women are breadwinners. At Fufore and St Theresa's, women farm the land, growing vegetables and some other crops. They sell their produce at police and army checkpoints where they think they are safe from attacks. We met Grace Malgwi, who shared a deeply touching story of how she was sexually assaulted by her captors and was abandoned to die in the bush. She was rescued by a good Samaritan who took her to a nearby community, where she regained her strength and eventually found her way to St Theresa's.

Pilgrims also met with the executive governor of Adamawa State, His Excellency Senator Jibrilla Bindow. We were received by the governor and his executive cabinet at the Government House. The PTV spokesperson brought the challenging conditions of IDPs—especially the health and educational services—to the attention of the governor. Issues concerning insecurity in some parts of the state, and the desire of IDPs to return to their native homes, were also shared with the governor. The team called on the government to support the establishment and resourcing of the Adamawa State Inter-Religious Council. The governor assured the team that all the issues tabled would be addressed. Other persons visited were the President of the Lutheran World Federation, Dr Musa Panti Filibus; the Paramount Traditional ruler of Numan kingdom, the Hama Bachama; and His Royal Majesty Homun

Honest Stephen Irmiya. We attended a worship service at the Cathedral of the Lutheran Church of Christ in Nigeria, along with over 4000 people.

Women's Situation in Nigeria

The following points summarize some of the negative aspects of Nigerian women's lives, as told to and observed by the pilgrims.

- Women and children are the main victims of existing conflicts. Women are the ones who usually work on the land and are often victims of clashes over land.

- When men are killed in attacks, women become breadwinners while still continuing to care for children, the elderly, and the maimed.

- In Boko Haram attacks, women and girls are targeted, killed, raped, and enslaved.

- Women who are abducted to Boko Haram camps experience negative physical health and psychological status. Young girls are influenced by harmful practices, wrong models of leadership, and exclusion.

- Women do not have ready access to leadership positions in most Nigerian churches.

- All human rights of women, especially those who are victims of conflicts, are grossly violated.

- The government of Nigeria launched the National Action Plan on Women, Peace and Security; in practice, however, most women working in difficult places and circumstances lack protection. They are stereotyped and they face harmful practices and negative attitudes that exclude them from community life. This is especially true for those who have been traumatized.

- Women who have lost their husbands are deprived of their property and house; they are forced into marriage to save their lives and the lives of their children.

- Women and children make up the greatest share of the population in IDP camps. They are taught some skills but are not granted capital to start businesses. There is gender insensitivity in the provision of certain services in the camps. Women and girls in the camps are vulnerable to rape by security officials.

- Children lack access to quality education.

- Women bear the brunt of violent conflicts but are denied the opportunity of participating in decision-making. Some women are radicalized and want revenge for the way they have been treated.

- Women and girls suffer silently because culture and traditions deny them a voice. Many children and women battle trauma because of what they have experienced.

The pilgrims also heard stories of women's efforts—against the odds—to deepen peace.

- Christian and Muslim women are working together for peace and peaceful co-existence.

- Women's civil society groups are proactively teaching their children to respect, accept, and be tolerant of others, regardless of religious conviction.

- Peace clubs are being formed in schools.

- Young people are being trained in relationship skills, confidence building, and trauma healing.

- There is a campaign against gender-based violence.

- A commissioner of women's rights was appointed in Plateau State.

- A media campaign and other efforts are increasing awareness of peacebuilding.

The women's Pilgrim Team Visit was a transformative journey, an awakening to the needs of others and the vision of God. It was a summons to a new way of life and a transformative spirituality of justice and peace. The experience was significant because journeying with vulnerable groups and becoming vulnerable oneself helps to purge one's own prejudices, preoccupations, and priorities. "One God of life, one creation; one humanity calling the one church of Jesus Christ to commitment and engagement where peace and justice are threatened"[1] also in Nigeria.

---

1. "Pilgrimage of Justice and Peace," WCC Website, https://www.oikoumene.org/uk/taxonomy/term/2236.

Recommendations for the Future

The following are recommendations for peacebuilding in Nigeria:

- Everyone, including marginalized groups, deserves to be treated well. Churches should avoid attitudes and comments that lead to marginalization. They should understand that reconciliation is healing therapy for all and sundry.

- Everyone involved in conflicts and affected by destruction has to be involved in the processes of building peace. People need courage and opportunities to speak up. Churches are in better positions to create such opportunities. Relationships need to be repaired and institutions need to be reformed. All factions—especially religious groups that are directly or indirectly involved in many of the conflicts—should play leading roles in entrenching values that will steer the people of Nigeria towards a sustainable and peaceful future.

- The road to recovery will be long for the affected individuals, communities, regions, and the nation. The cultural and structural conditions that generate deadly or destructive disagreements must be transformed. Preaching love rather than hate, and Christ rather than ethnicity, can lead to the hope-for end.

- Religion serves as the foundation of many cultural norms and values. Christianity, for instance, addresses the most profound existential issues of human life. Christian religious teaching and practices ought to support peace, social justice, reconciliation, and harmony. Churches should be committed to using every avenue to teach such spiritual and moral principles.

- Churches should take the lead in facilitating peace agreements. They should provide safe spaces for conversation between contending parties and outreach to rebel and disaffected groups. They should work directly with the victims of war.

- Faith-based organizations should pay attention to the relationships between people and groups. This will enable them to provide early warning signals of deterioration of peace among people. In this way, peacebuilding becomes the concern of every member of the community.

4

Reflections on the Peacebuilding Response in Nigeria

Ephraim Yakubu Simon

Africa's most populous country, Nigeria, can be described as a quintessence of diversity. The country has an estimated population of over 200 million and an annual growth rate of 2.61 per cent. Nigeria has more than 250 ethnic groups. Besides its multi-ethnic nature, religious diversity is also one of the distinct features of Nigeria. Although Islam and Christianity are the two main religions in the country, there are also some Nigerians who are adherents of African Traditional Religion. The people and groups that make up Nigeria's rich cultural heritage coexisted peacefully until the beginning of the 21st century when the country started experiencing interethnic and interreligious conflict.

Nigeria, especially the northern part, has become a conflict-ridden environment. Issues of displacement and insecurity have negatively impacted agricultural and livestock farming. Value chains have been disrupted, and the rural population's capacity for self-sufficiency has diminished. Farmers and cattle herders compete over natural resources such as water and land. Pressure on natural resources has increased continuously in recent years due to the population boom, while climate change has resulted in increased movement of cattle herders from northern to central Nigeria. In addition, the expansion of agricultural land and settlements has led to a reduction in the availability of pastureland; agricultural policies have made the situation of pastoralists even more complex and challenging. As a result, traditional conflict management mechanisms and agreements have not been maintained. Disputes over damaged crops, polluted water, degraded land, livestock theft, terrorism, kidnapping for ransom, and crimes against humanity are on the rise. The ensuing conflicts frequently end with violence.[1]

The lack of economic and employment opportunities, particularly for young people, is an important factor contributing to restlessness, and this

---

1. "Strengthening Capacities for Peacebuilding and Conflict Resolution in Nigeria's Middle Belt," Deutsche Gesellschaft für Internationale Zusammenarbeit (GIZ), last updated December 2020, https://www.giz.de/en/worldwide/93607.html.

has made young people vulnerable to recruitment into armed groups. The northern states of Nigeria have low rates of literacy and youth employment compared to the southern part of the country. Communities across the region face both immediate and long-term effects of socio-economic conflict, including violence, drug abuse, criminality, and terrorism. The violence in Nigeria has drastically increased the number of orphans and widows in the country. Thousands of children have been orphaned and are living in deplorable conditions.2 This situation has negatively affected the mission and ministry of the church.

The Nigerian churches have a long history of responding to the security challenges that continue to menace Nigerian societies. Churches have promoted peace and reconciliation in Nigeria with a special focus on the northern states. They continue to appeal to the conscience of the people using religious teachings, while also responding to the humanitarian crisis and providing psychosocial accompaniment to the affected within the communities. This gesture from the Nigerian churches can be traced back to the Nigerian civil war (1967–70) and many other conflicts within the country.

The invitation from the 10th Assembly of the World Council of Churches (WCC), calling on churches and people of good will to join in the pilgrimage of justice and peace, was well received by the churches in Nigeria. To me, it was a wake-up call to the churches to stand up to their responsibility and strengthen their peacebuilding engagement in a society bedevilled by insecurity. In response to the invitation, I have seen churches visiting affected communities and celebrating the faithfulness of God, while prophetically challenging the injustice that has widened the scope of insecurity in the nation. The response of the churches was amplified during the COVID-19 pandemic lockdown in 2020.

Reflection on the Nigerian Churches' Engagement in the Peacebuilding Process Since the Busan Assembly

The 10th assembly of the WCC took place in Busan, Republic of South Korea, from 30 October to 8 November 2013, with the theme "God of Life, Lead Us to Justice and Peace." The message of the assembly focused on the central words "common pilgrimage." It was to be a pilgrimage of transformation

---

2. "Food Security, Nigeria, Our Stories," World Renew, 4 May 2016, https://worldrenew.net/our-stories/healing-from-trauma-and-promoting-peace-in-nigeria.

for all those involved in order that they might become instruments of peace. The message called on the churches to be devoted to achieving justice and peace for all, irrespective of colour, race, ethnicity, or religion. Churches were encouraged to join in this common journey from their own contexts to bring about peace and reconciliation for all. Furthermore, the assembly appealed to churches to do more to protect nature and to respond to the global economic crisis, as well as to other socio-political and spiritual challenges.

To demonstrate the urgency and the importance of this invitation, the WCC leadership, led by then-general secretary Rev. Dr Olav Fykse Tveit, visited Nigeria in 2016. During this visit, an interfaith centre founded jointly by the Christian Council of Nigeria (CCN) and Jama'tul Nasril Islam (JNI), and supported by the WCC, was inaugurated. There was a follow-up of the Pilgrim Team Visit (PTV) to Nigeria in February 2017, and later that year a women's PTV, "Walking Her Stories," was led by the WCC moderator Dr Agnes Abuom and Rev. Cornelia Füllkrug-Weitzel. The CCN and the churches of Nigeria hosted these visits. The common elements of these PTVs were visits to affected communities, celebration of the different gifts and resilience of these communities in the face of violent conflicts and challenging the injustices against humanity with calls to leaders to rise to their responsibilities of protecting lives and property. This, to me, was a boost to the Nigerian churches and the CCN as they continued to accompany the communities affected by the crisis—the traumatized, the women, the orphans, and other affected persons. The Peace and Trauma Healing Centre located at the Institute of Church and Society, Jos, and the Joint CCN and JNI Interfaith Centre in Kaduna have educated and sensitized churches on community peacebuilding efforts and have worked in schools and with young people. They have used the media to counter hate speech and to encourage churches to show greater religious tolerance. Traditional and religious leaders, women, and young people are actively engaged in these efforts in Nigeria, with a special focus on northern Nigeria.

One key lesson during the women's PTV to Nigeria was the invitation to lift up women's visibility in peacebuilding in Nigeria. The visit created space for women to share their stories of trauma, pain, victory, and resilience in the face of challenges they had experienced. It was also an opportunity to interact with different stakeholders, churches, mosques, political office holders, traditional rulers, and society. The visit was like a spark to women's consciousness to rise up to challenge the injustices in society. Since then, women and youth have been more visible. They have engaged in peacebuilding, addressing the increased rate of gender-based violence and issues of rape in society. The church leaders, including women and youth, have been more active by speaking out against injustices and the lack of political will of the political leadership to end these atrocities. They have continued to provide pastoral accompaniment and support to families whose loved ones were kidnapped, including efforts to secure the release of the captives. I see these actions as being motivated and strengthened by our common pilgrimage of justice and peace.

A summary of this reflection

Amid the challenges, pains, and traumas that the people of Nigeria are facing due to violent conflict, the church has remained a beacon of hope in the matter of peacebuilding.

The various Pilgrim Team Visits assured Nigerians of the solidarity of the global fellowship with the churches and people of Nigeria. This has empowered and strengthened the churches to remain committed to and engaged in peacebuilding in Nigeria.

Women's voices were strengthened and are now visible in the public domain because of the women's PTV. Today women from our churches and the CCN are engaged by public and private media to speak on the issues of security, gender-based violence, and rape. The Women's Wing of the Christian Council of Nigeria is a strong voice in Nigeria today.

Interfaith relationships and collaboration have been strengthened between Christians and Muslims with the space created through the International Centre for Interfaith Peace and Harmony (ICIPH) in Kaduna.

The civil society organizations, NGOs, and faith-based organizations—for instance, Justice, Peace and Reconciliation Movement (JPRM), Peace and Trauma Healing Centre located at the Institute of Church and Society Jos, and TEKAN Peace Desk—which coordinated the women's PTV in 2017, took this visit very seriously. They have since then been more engaged in peacebuilding activities to ensure a just, peaceful, and humane world. The visit was a great opportunity for us to learn. We have since then done lots more peacebuilding work, such as: women's engagement in peace and security issues, women's empowerment, community building, Christian-Muslim dialogue, interactive media programs, conflict prevention strategies, interreligious and intercultural dialogue, trauma healing, and conflict monitoring (including early warning and early response, humanitarian response, and intervention).

The Pilgrimage of Justice and Peace Harvest Workshop on the Priority Countries

I was privileged to participate and share experiences from the Nigerian context on the responses of the Nigerian church and the CCN on the security situation in Nigeria. I am happy to reflect again on two major contributions of the churches since the WCC 10th Assembly, including the establishment of the Peace and Trauma Healing Centre located at the Institute of Church and Society Jos (PTHC-ICS) and the International Centre for Interfaith Peace and Harmony located in Kaduna. Knowing fully that this workshop was aimed at harvesting our achievements and challenges in our common journey from Busan on our way to Karlsruhe, we shared these major achievements as our success stories from Nigeria.

PTHC-ICS

It has often been said that prevention is better than cure: hence the decision of the CCN to establish the ICS-PTHC to respond to the devastating effects of armed violence on the people of Nigeria in the peacebuilding journey. We felt that providing psychosocial accompaniment to victims of terrorism and armed conflicts is an integral part of countering violent extremism. Many victims of armed conflict are likely to suffer severe emotional trauma that may affect their ability to develop emotional awareness, empathy, self-esteem, and basic problem-solving skills. If left unchecked, many of these victims grow up believing that violence is the only way to cope; as a result, many of them become vulnerable to extremist viewpoints. As the director of the centre, I have observed from years of working with victims that the common symptoms of the effects of violence include social withdrawal, loss of appetite, aggression, anxiety, depression, and flashbacks that trigger nightmares. Therefore, one of the most effective ways to defeat terrorism and banditry, as is the case in Nigeria, is to promote peacebuilding activities and effective trauma counselling.

The centre has been doing this through training of lay trauma counsellors, training of community peace agents, holding trauma sessions with various IDP centres, economically empowering victims of conflicts with a special focus on women, providing humanitarian support to victims of conflicts, and creating spaces for story and experience sharing by the victims. From my experience in the field, I agree with the statement that trauma healing programs do not only provide a helpful forum for traumatized individuals to share and learn, but they also help to create a foundation for forgiveness in communities.3 As people openly discuss stories of painful experiences, they also have the chance to discuss methods of promoting forgiveness and peace as they work for healing. At the end of a trauma healing workshop, one of the participants said, "I am grateful to God for the trauma healing program, and it has greatly encouraged me to move on in life and forgive the attackers who destroyed my home and possessions. The program has been timely and medicinal in my life." We receive testimonies like this daily.

ICIPH

The CCN and the JNI jointly established the International Centre for Interfaith Peace and Harmony (ICIPH). The joint effort was an outcome of a high-level international interfaith fact-finding mission to Nigeria led by the WCC and the Royal Jordanian Aal Al-Bayt Institute of Islamic Thought. The ICIPH has contributed to the process of peace by promoting justice and reconciliation between Christians and Muslims, with particular emphasis on the northern states, a region that has experienced many violent conflicts since 2002. Since its inception in 2016, the centre has served as a safe space for Muslim and Christian engagement, providing peacebuilding training and convening joint activities focusing on religious leaders, women, youth, and young schoolchildren. Furthermore, the ICIPH is seen as a platform that has successfully brought together local and international faith-based agencies and experts in conflict transformation to address interfaith relationships in Nigeria in collaboration with quasi-governmental organizations, the United Nations Development Programme, and national and international NGOs.

Activities such as Hand Across the Divide, training and recruitment of peace ambassadors and peace vanguards, Train-the-Trainer workshops for ICIPH Peace Ambassadors, Train-the-Trainer workshops on neighbourhood security, sensitization of youth on the peaceful conduct of elections, sensitization on peace for secondary school students, and activation of peace clubs in secondary schools have contributed to visible cooperation among the two religions in northern Nigeria.

The Pilgrimage Harvest workshop was not only a platform to share experiences on the peacebuilding work in Nigeria from Busan to Karlsruhe. For me, it was also an opportunity to learn about how other churches in other contexts are responding to our common pilgrimage of justice and peace. I was so fascinated by the experiences of the DRC and Burundi. These encouraged

---

3. See "Food Security, Nigeria, Our Stories," World Renew.

me and strengthened my commitment to engage more on the journey of a just peace in Nigeria.

Practical Steps Churches Can Take Going Forward

Member churches can no longer open their doors, wait, and expect that people will come in. Effective congregations go into the world to encounter those in need of the gospel.

- The religious leaders are the closest to the citizens at the grassroots. They have closer influence and should therefore bear the burden of living in peace and preaching peace. They should *not* promote hate speech from the pulpit.

- Going forward, the WCC, through the Pilgrimage of Justice and Peace, should accompany churches, helping them to invest more in women and young people in capacity-building opportunities within and outside their local zones.

- Churches are present in even the most remote communities; the church should, therefore, be the voice of the people and enable communities to interface with the government and other outside help.

- The church should assist community members by helping them to look inward for ways to identify simple and local solutions for the challenges they face.

The Need for Peacebuilding in Iraq and the Church's Role in the Process

Emanuel Youkhana

Background

At a time when the ethno-religious and cultural diversity of the Iraqi people is rich, every component of this diversity adds value that continues throughout history in all areas of subsistence, community, economic and otherwise. However, because of the accumulation of policies of persecution, exclusion, and discrimination practised in Iraq against minorities, this diversity is threatened. Many of the original and indigenous Iraqi communities are facing an existential threat.

Diversity is a cause of enrichment, but it has become a cause of mass murder and displacement.

The genocide, mass killings, and systematic terror practised by ISIS in Iraq against Yazidis and Christians in 2014 was not the beginning but rather a continuation of centuries-old policies that did not change with the formation of the contemporary Iraqi state after World War I and have continued with various successive regimes ruling contemporary Iraq.

The systematic destruction of the Assyrians in the region of Semele in 1933, from which the term *genocide* was coined by Raphael Lemkin, was the beginning that later continued in the pogrom against Jews (1941), Al-Anfal against Kurds and Assyrians, and the crimes against Shiites in southern Iraq, and many other mass crimes. All these successive persecutions have created a legislative, cultural, educational, and societal atmosphere that tolerates and even justifies the persecution, discrimination, and abolition of the other.

These accumulations and atmosphere, as well as external factors related to the Middle East region in general, and the interests and interventions of external countries, have provided the background and ability for ISIS to commit the most heinous crime of genocide of the century.

The consequences of ISIS terrorism are not limited to the human and material losses suffered by Yazidis and Christians but have gone beyond it to tear apart the diverse community fabric, posing a future and existential threat to the cohesion of the Iraqi community.

How can there be a future for a nation if it is not cohesive? For this future, and for our future generations, we must work hard to build peaceful coexistence among the diverse communities of the Iraqi people.

The various state institutions are directly responsible for peacebuilding, and they will be able to do so if they have awareness, will, and decision. To that end, Iraqi Christian churches have a vital and influential role to play. While many are seeking to build walls, churches are seeking to build bridges.

What is this peaceful coexistence that we need?

Peaceful coexistence is not just a nice and attractive term by which we address feelings and emotions. Are there those who do not want to live and coexist? Are there those who do not want peace and safe? So, is there anyone who doesn't want to live peacefully?

Peaceful coexistence is not statements and words on platforms and in the media. Peaceful coexistence in the case of Iraq should be a government and community program and action plan aimed at restoring the destroyed bridges and the trust that has become lost among the components of the Iraqi people.

It is not enough for victims of organized violence and terrorism to listen to beautiful statements and statements they must see actions on the ground. Despite the importance of physical reconstruction, material compensation and the reconstruction of property, infrastructure, and services are not sufficient for the victims. Most of all, the collective memory should be addressed, and the roots of the problem should be fixed to prevent recurrence. The victims who lost a lot, including their dignity, cannot live as prisoners of memory. This memory must be healed if we are to build a common future that guarantees individual and collective dignity on the principle of equality, justice, and mutual respect—so that future generations of vulnerable communities and minorities feel that they live in their homeland and have their voice and participation in the building of their homeland.

To heal the memory and restore peaceful coexistence, more than one level must be worked on, including legislative, executive, judicial, media, and educational. We must all participate in this process: the state, civil society, religious groups, and others.

Ecclesiastical Calls for Civil Peace and National Reconciliation

The Eastern Christian churches, as in the rest of the troubled regions of the world, has played an important role, with a voice that has resonated in times of crisis, particularly existential ones. Their voice has always been visionary and oriented to the future, addressing the wounds of the past and the present. The church's voice and prayers are always to reunite, build bridges and unite people, turning away from sectarian and denominational interests and conflicts.

The role of Iraqi churches at the current stage is on the same track, with the same objectives. From the first days following the events of 2014, during the displacement phase, and in the healing and recovery phase that is ongoing, the Church has committed itself to calls and action programs for peaceful coexistence among Iraqi components. These may be calls for government agencies to undertake initiatives, meetings, programs, and action plans to bring together the dispersed. Or the Church may work at the grassroots level through programs and workshops in which young people of different affiliations, identities, and backgrounds participate.

The initiative of the government and the Church in Iraq to invite Pope Francis to visit Iraq in March 2021 was a historic step in the path of peaceful coexistence between Iraqi ethno-religious and cultural communities. His Holiness's visit and program, which included recognition and presence of marginalized Iraqi groups, was a picture of a true Iraq rich in diversity. It offered a picture of what a future Iraq should be. The joint prayer in Ur of Abraham, Father of believers, is a message that transcends its geographical boundaries. It goes beyond the identities of its participants in Iraqi communities to the religious and cultural identities of the diverse Middle East.

The historic fraternal meeting between His Holiness and The Eminence of the Supreme Shiite Authority Ayatollah Sistani in Najaf complemented the meeting between His Holiness and the Grand Sheikh of al-Azhar in the United Arab Emirates. It led to the signing of the "Document on Human Fraternity for World Peace and Living Together."1 The Iraqi government adopted the date of the meeting and designated March 6 as an annual Iraqi day of national tolerance. In 2022, this day served to launch a national diversity management

1. Andrea Tornielli, "Pope and the Grand Imam: Historic Declaration of Peace, Freedom, Women's Rights," Vatican News, 4 February 2019, https://www.vaticannews.va/en/pope/news/2019-02/pope-francis-uae-grand-imam-declaration-of-peace.html.

strategy program to further the path of healing in Iraq.

Church efforts were not limited to these initiatives. Church institutions and authorities, in cooperation with Iraqi civil society institutions, launched and implemented practical programs that contribute to peaceful coexistence. Among the most important of these initiatives was the work of the World Council of Churches (WCC) to organize two Iraqi interfaith conferences in Beirut, one held in December 2019 and the other in December 2021. Here where the diverse ethnic and religious communities gathered to exchange visions and prepare programs of action to enhance the role of religious authorities and institutions in establishing peaceful coexistence in Iraq.

One of the fruits of the first conference was the preparation of a program to review the Iraqi curriculum to include and positively reflect the religious and cultural diversity in Iraq. The WCC, in partnership with the NGO Christian Aid Program—Nohadra—Iraq (CAPNI) as a local implementing partner, completed this program over the past year. In addition, an educational guide for teachers was prepared. It also reflects Iraq's religious and cultural diversity and furthers the spirit of the human fraternity agreement between the Vatican and Al-Azhar.

Recommendations

Despite the importance of previous steps, there is more work to be done. Perhaps the most important of these are the following:

- Review of the constitution and Iraqi legislation and laws in force to achieve non-discrimination between Iraqi communities on the basis of religion or race. This forms the basis for building a state of citizenship, a state that we all dream to reach.

- Adoption of legislation and programs to publicize Iraqi diversity in governmental, community, and public spaces through curricula, media, awareness campaigns, and other avenues.

- Application of transitional justice,[2] not only to guarantee the rights of victims, but also to reassure younger generations that the phase of tolerance for persecution is over.

- Formation of a council of Iraqi churches in which all Iraqi churches are represented.

---

2. This is a term used often in the context of the Middle East, especially in Iraq. It calls to accountability all those who committed war crimes in order to transit into peace, you cannot achieve peace without transitional justice.

- Formation and support of an Iraqi platform in which the religious affiliations of all Iraqi communities are represented.

- Investing in young people through youth programs that are national, trans-religious, and trans-regional to cover all religious spectrums and Iraqi geography.

The wounds are deep.

The collective memory is painful.

The path is long.

But there must be a beginning.

By then, the future is bright.

The Path Toward Healing, Reconciliation, and Peace in the Korean Peninsula

Seung-min Shin

Overview of the Peacebuilding Process Since the 10th Assembly of the WCC in Busan

In the "Statement on Peace and Reunification of the Korean Peninsula" of the Busan Assembly,[1] the World Council of Churches (WCC) reaffirmed its firm commitment to stand in solidarity with the Christians in the North and South, especially with the Korean churches' faithful actions towards the peace, healing, reconciliation, and reunification of their people and their land.

Since then, the WCC has faithfully committed to peacebuilding on the Korean Peninsula. In 2013, 2015, and 2018, general secretary Rev. Dr Olav Fykse Tveit visited Seoul and Pyongyang, meeting with President Moon Jae-in of South Korea and Chairman Kim Jong-un of North Korea. He encouraged the political leaders to play a leading role in the Korean peace process. In addition, with the facilitation of the WCC Commission of the Churches on International Affairs, church leaders from the South and North were able to meet at least seven times on the Korean Peninsula (in Pyongyang in 2015) as well as in Geneva, China, and Thailand. In particular, on the 70th anniversary of the WCC in June 2018, the meeting between Pope Francis and the church leaders from South and North was a powerful and touching event, making the church visible as an agent for peace and reconciliation.

In addition to the efforts among the leaders, there were grassroots actions organized by young people and women. As a part of the Pilgrimage of Justice and Peace in Asia, about 100 young people from the WCC and the Ecumenical Youth Council in Korea gathered in South Korea for a week to articulate their vision for peace and reaffirm their commitment to peacebuilding in the world. In 2020, the WCC's Women of Faith Pilgrim Team had an online joint program with Korean church women. Furthermore, the WCC and the

---

1. Statement on Peace and Reunification of the Korean Peninsula. Adopted by the WCC 10th Assembly as part of the Report of the Public Issues Committee.

National Council of Churches in Korea (NCCK) organized a peace prayer movement, "The Light of Peace—Churches in Solidarity with the Korean Peninsula," from 1 March to 31 August 2020 and published a book with 70 prayers and stories from the movement.

These peacebuilding initiatives of Korean churches and the WCC are grassroots efforts to implement the commitments expressed in the 10th Assembly's statement on peace and reunification on the Korean Peninsula.

Reflection on Churches' Engagement in the Peacebuilding Process

"The Centre of Our Mission"

Following is a list of peacebuilding activities undertaken by Korean churches since the 10th Assembly of the WCC in Busan.

- Leaders of the churches in the North and South have continually met through the Ecumenical Forum for Peace, Reunification, and Cooperation on the Korean Peninsula.

- The Korean churches took an initiative for healing and unity by declaring a peace treaty for the Korean Peninsula in a ceremony organized by the Presbyterian Church in the Republic of Korea on 20 June 2020.

- The DMZ Human Chain Movement, organized by churches and civil society in Korea in 2019, was a joyous occasion, in which a "human chain" of 500,000 people was formed along the 500-kilometre Demilitarized Zone. That grassroots movement was a reminder that transformation is an essential dimension of the kingdom of God. Holding each other's hands to seek the transformation of the DMZ into a peace zone, as outlined in the Panmunjom Declaration for Peace, Prosperity, and Reunification of the Korean Peninsula, is the beginning of our journey.

- A peace convocation, coordinated by the Presbyterian Church in the Republic of Korea was held on 20 June 2020 at the White Horse Hill Memorial in Cholwon. People held blue umbrellas as a symbol of unity, as they prayed, walked, and called for peace together. In this important witness for peace, churches are committed and determined to pursue the Christian calling to be peacemakers, the vision of peaceful coexistence between North and South, and ultimately the reunification of the long-divided Korean people.

- In 2020, as an ecumenical expression of both lament and hope, the churches in Korea and the WCC launched a 70-day global prayer campaign, "We Pray, Peace Now, End the War," from 1 March to 15 August 2020. It was an important point in our ecumenical Pilgrimage of Justice and Peace, as we invited all Christians to deepen their relationship with God and each other by joining in prayer for the formal end to the Korean War and the replacement of the Armistice Agreement with a permanent peace treaty. The prayer campaign represented our vision, hope, and dedication, not just for peace on the Korean Peninsula, but for peace for the whole world.

- In response to the Korean churches' efforts for peace, on 25 June 2020—the 70th anniversary of the start of the Korean War—the WCC issued a peace message expressing a strong commitment to peace in the northeast Asian region and throughout the world and appealing for an end to the threat of military action and for peace on the Korean Peninsula.

- A Declaration for the People's Korea Peace Agreement was launched on 23 July 2020, initiated by the NCCK and civil organizations in Korea. Churches and people in Korea are seeking a new era through a peace agreement, campaigning not only in Korea but also in neighbouring countries and the US. People around the world have sent support and pledged solidarity with this struggle.

Despite these efforts, inter-Korea relations, which improved in 2018, are deteriorating again. Moreover, the worsening relationship between China and the USA, and the Ukrainian war, are driving international support for the Korea peace process to the margins. Opportunities for trust-building between North and South Korea have completely disappeared, as the inter-Korean exchanges and areas of cooperation have dwindled drastically since 2020. This in turn is increasing the hostility between North and South. Church has been no exception. Many South Korean churches are still hostile toward North Korea, casting doubts on the efforts of the ecumenical community (such as NCCK) to achieve peace and reconciliation. What has gone wrong?

The division system is the source of the greatest pain upon the land and people of the Korean Peninsula. But this division, the root cause of all pains, has not been the centre of our mission. Jeong Se-hoon, a Korean poet, says in his poem "The Centre of the Body":

> To the center of the body the mind goes to not hurt to touch it
>
> The center of the body is not the thinking brain nor is it the brea-thing lungs
>
> Nor is it the heart pumping blood
>
> The place in pain! Where you cannot help but touch the wounded place
>
> To that place our whole mind is moving.[2]

As the very place in pain is the centre of our body, so the suffering places in the world must be the centre of our mission. The unity we seek in the ecumenical movement must not be found in the places of power and glory, but in the places of division and conflict, suffering and pain, discrimination and hatred, and marginalization and alienation.

Lessons from the Ecumenical Efforts in the Peace Process on the Korean Peninsula

> Where there is no vision, the people perish.
>
> —Proverbs 29:18 (KJV)

During the hot summer in 2019, about 100 young people came and gathered at the DMZ. The week-long Pilgrimage of Justice and Peace workshop was a great inspiration to all participants. The overseas participants saw and felt the pains of the divided country with their full bodies and spirits, as those pains have left unhealed marks everywhere in South Korea.

One of the young participants from the United States shared her eye-opening moments: "I didn't fully realize that the Korean War has not ended. During our journey, North Korea even launched two ballistic missiles into the East Sea as an armed demonstration in response to ongoing military exercises. Both places of pilgrimage, to Nogeun-ri and the DMZ, gave me a special lesson that healing for wounds and victims is the key issue in Korea. I witnessed a great desire and hope for peace and reunification." These personal experiences empowered the young people with the creative imagination and concrete initiatives for peace-building and solidarity.

---

2. Jeong Se-hoon, MomeuiJoongsim [The Centre of the Body], (Seoul: Samchang, 2016), 26–27.

The workshop held during the harvest gathering on 10–11 June 2021 was a time to share experiences from the Pilgrimage of Justice and Peace from different contexts, such as Nigeria, South Sudan, the Democratic Republic of Congo, Burundi, Palestine and Israel, and the Korean Peninsula. An important lesson learned from the workshop is that each country's experiences, challenges, and opportunities are resonant and cross-over in the journey of peace-building. We should solidify the international bonds in the journey of the peace process.

Practical Recommendations

The Korean War has not ended yet. After the tragic three-year war, an Armistice, not a peace agreement was signed. July 2023 marks the 70th anniversary of the Armistice. During the last seven decades, the Korean people have suffered so much, hating, and killing each other. 70 years is enough. Now it is time to end the hostility and war.

In 2020, more than 400 religious and civil NGOs joined together to launch the "Korea Peace Appeal Campaign" to end the Korean War and initiate a true Korean peace agreement. This campaign will continue until July 2023. The NCCK is urging its member churches and overseas partner churches to join in the campaign to gather one million signatures by 2023. We imagine a future where the people of the Korean Peninsula, East Asia, and the world cooperate and coexist peacefully. We hope our resources will be used for people's safety and happiness, for environmental sustainability, and for a society without discrimination—instead of for war preparations. Please join us in the Korea Peace Appeal Campaign.

QR link to the
Peace Appeal

Reflecting on the theme of the upcoming WCC assembly in Karlsruhe, "Christ's Love Moves the World to Reconciliation and Unity," I suggest that after this assembly, Korean churches and people and the WCC should take the following steps to further the peace process on the Korean Peninsula:

- Continue to strengthen the ecumenical bonds for peace and reunification on the Korean Peninsula by reaching more ecumenical partners in the context of the Ecumenical Forum for Peace, Reunification, and Cooperation on the Korean Peninsula

- Continue to hold the cooperation between churches in Korea and the US as a framework for the discussion of multilateral missions for peace and reunification on the Korean Peninsula

- Create a Nordic round table for peace and reunification on the Korean Peninsula

7

Pilgrimage of Justice and Peace: Come and See and Act

Munib A. Younan

I am very grateful for the initiative of the World Council of Churches (WCC) in calling for the Pilgrimage of Justice and Peace. As I live in Jerusalem, the city of pilgrimage, I have known since childhood that pilgrims come to experience the places where Jesus was born, taught, was crucified, raised from the dead, and ascended into heaven. I have known that just as there is a history and theology of salvation, there is also a geography of salvation. The events of Jesus' life happened in a real place and in real time.

Pilgrims come and go, experiencing this holy geography for a short time, but we who live in Jerusalem go about our daily lives. Sometimes we may not fully appreciate the holiness of this city. Occasionally, it is a pilgrim who visits us and reminds us of the unique and holy nature of this place. My father used to tell me that in the early 20th century when Russian pilgrims came to the holy land, they would remain barefoot until they departed. I also think of the Orthodox Cypriots who would visit Jerusalem. They opted to stay in the homes of Palestinian Christians and would ask if there were any unbaptized children they could become godparents for. Their faces were filled with joy when someone would call them *hajji* or "pilgrim."

The churches in Jerusalem have learned much from these pilgrims over the years. For one thing, pilgrimage is not a one-way street. Pilgrimage works in both directions. Yes, pilgrims come to revive their own faith, to seek a deeper understanding of the Bible, and to experience the living Christ. They come to be with the local church and people, to listen, to worship, and to hear their stories. But at the same time, when local Christians receive pilgrims, they are also enriched and deeply affected by the experience. Pilgrimage is therefore a mutual transformation for the ones who have travelled far and for the ones who have received those travellers.

The ecumenical family in Jerusalem appreciates that the WCC, under the leadership of former general secretary Olav Fykse Tveit, has developed this concept of a pilgrimage of justice and peace. This is an invitation for Christians to walk and work together toward a common goal, renewing the true vocation of the church as co-creators of the kingdom of God on earth as in heaven. This collaboration toward the goal of justice and peace is how we together can heal the world of injustice, conflict, oppression, occupation, colonialism, and threats to the environment.

Christians are aware that today, the very world is in peril from poverty, economic injustice, violence, and ecological disaster. We have heard today that 80 per cent of religious persecutions in the world are against Christians. Those who are oppressed or persecuted do not need words or statements but ask for the involvement of their brothers and sisters in Christ in their struggle for freedom and justice. Such grave dangers can drain our hope. For this reason, pilgrimage is essential in our peacebuilding. We support one another through the mutual transformation that comes from pilgrimage.

Pilgrimage is essential for two theological reasons:

1. Pilgrimage is an integral part of the theology of incarnation. The manger of the baby born in Bethlehem reminds us of God's pilgrimage into this broken world. It would have been simpler for God the Creator to speak a word and heal the world. But God opted rather to be born among us, in the humblest of circumstances, in order to be involved with us. Jesus Christ, God incarnate, chose to be among the locals, to walk where we walk, to know our sufferings and our joys. He was hungry and thirsty like us. He offered healing and hope to all, and in the end was betrayed and denied and crucified. Jesus knew well the brokenness of the human being. And still, he chose to walk with us, to love us, even to forgive us from the cross. His whole life was a pilgrimage of justice and peace.

2. Communion *(Koinonia)* among Christians cannot be achieved through issuing good statements, receiving excellent media coverage, or creating savvy social media posts. True communion comes through accompaniment, following the example of the walk to Emmaus. We truly know one another—and we know the risen Christ—when we walk together, hear one another's stories, and share a common life, even if for a short time. Only by walking together and breaking bread together can we strengthen each other and work together toward the mutual goals of justice and peace. Our faith is revived when we encounter the steadfastness of those on the margins: when we allow ourselves to become vulnerable

and embrace the vulnerability of others. Pilgrimage is not tourism, nor is it a vacation. It is a journey of mutual spiritual transformation.

The WCC's Pilgrimage of Justice and Peace to Israel and Palestine is not a new invention. The WCC and the church leaders in Jerusalem established the Ecumenical Accompaniment Programme in Palestine and Israel (EAPPI) and the Jerusalem Interchurch Centre together in 2002. The idea was that the member churches of the WCC would accompany the churches of Jerusalem and its institutions, providing a protective presence and advocating for justice and an end to the occupation. EAPPI created accompaniers who understand the stories of both sides in an objective way. Now EAPPI has over 1600 ambassadors from different countries and nationalities. As with the pilgrimage mentioned above, this was not a one-sided learning trip: it was a mutual transformation for all involved. We have come to see that the most eloquent statements of concern and solidarity can never do what walking together, eating together, and living together can accomplish. Therefore, come, see, and act. This kind of accompaniment strengthens and deepens our communion.

To further walk together on this road, I encourage the WCC to continue this practice of pilgrimage. This is the best path toward peace based on justice, and reconciliation based on forgiveness. The unity we seek emanates from these pilgrimages and creates a communion which includes everyone, especially those on the margins of society. May our living God continue to bless this initiative, and may God bless all pilgrims and those who receive them.

8

Overview of the Peacebuilding Process in South Sudan

James Oyet Latansio

The hope for peace and stability in South Sudan was restored when a peace pact—the Agreement on the Resolution of the Conflict in the Republic of South Sudan (ARCSS)—was signed between the Sudan People's Liberation Movement and Army in Government and SPLM/A in Opposition, as represented by President Salva Kiir Mayardit and First Vice President Dr Riek Machar Teny Dhurgon, respectively.

The agreement, which was signed in August 2015 in Addis Ababa, Ethiopia, and in Juba, South Sudan, was ratified by the South Sudan National Legislative Assembly on 10 September of that year. The agreement sought to end the deadly civil war that had broken out in South Sudan in December 2013, following power struggles between President Kiir and his deputy, Dr Machar. However, this accord was watered down in July 2016 when fighting broke out in the Presidential Palace. It was revitalized in September 2018 through another peace process facilitated by the Intergovernmental Authority on Development (IGAD).

The peacebuilding process in South Sudan relies on progress in implementing the Revitalized Agreement on the Resolution of the Conflict in South Sudan (R-ARCSS), which has been generally slow and inconsistent. The entire implementation process is behind schedule by almost the exact amount of time (16 months) so far spent on the transitional period. The transitional security arrangements in Chapter II of the Agreement were supposed to have been accomplished in the pre-transitional period, while the term of the Revitalized Transitional National Legislative Assembly should have started concurrently with that of the Revitalized Transitional Government of National Unity. This has had a considerable secondary effect on the implementation of the mandates of the security and legislative institutions in support of the peace implementation over this period.

Reflection on the South Sudan Council of Church's Engagement in the Peacebuilding Process

On 31 January 2014, immediately after the outbreak of violence in December 2013, the South Sudan Council of Churches (SSCC) Board of Trustees issued a pastoral exhortation, "Let Us Re-found Our Nation on a New Covenant," stressing the importance of ending the violence and conflict.

The most powerful action has been the SSCC Kigali Statement of Intent that was announced after SSCC Board of Trustees, Executive Committee, and Core Group Partners' retreat in Kigali, Rwanda, from the 1 to 7 June 2015. The aims of the retreat were to reflect on putting an end to the senseless war, the IGAD-initiated peace process, the experience of Rwanda after the stopping of the genocide, and trauma healing and reconciliation.

From the SSCC Kigali Statement of Intent, the SSCC developed a framework known as the Action Plan for Peace (APP) to end the war and resolve the conflict through a peacebuilding process. The SSCC APP has three major pillars: Advocacy (changing the narratives); Neutral Forum (creating spaces for community dialogues and conversations to rebuild trust and build confidence in peaceful coexistence); and Reconciliation. A fourth pillar is Capacity-Strengthening of the church leaders, to enhance peace, trauma healing, and reconciliation.

Workshop on the Priority Countries at the Pilgrimage of Justice and Peace Harvest Gathering

Since the 10th Assembly of the WCC in Busan, the SSCC has engaged the South Sudanese grassroots communities in peacebuilding, especially in Greater Jonglei State and Pibor Administrative Area (2020), and in Greater Tambura County in Western Equatoria State (December 2021). In these regions, sexual violence against women and girls, revenge and innocent killings of civilians, and cattle raids have taken deep roots. The WCC and the SSCC leadership embarked on a solidarity visit of hope, with community dialogues creating free spaces to talk about peace and reconciliation and reduce the circle of violence. The church leaders' solidarity visit increased the hope of the people in the community, who view the church as the only way out of the violence and their misery. However, the impact of the trauma of violence and abuse was felt by the church leaders during the visit. The solidarity visits to the respective areas were a response to grassroots community peace conversations. They were also the start of trauma healing through prayers and concrete signs of hope. These efforts and many others, such as the Anyuak Community Dialogue and Reconciliation in Pochalla, have been responses of the church in South Sudan in the work of peace, healing, justice, forgiveness, and reconciliation. I believe that the journey of peacebuilding through the Pilgrimage of Justice and Peace strengthens and supports the church and its leaders in the understanding of global ecumenical accompaniment toward a comprehensive and permanent peace and reconciliation. This also strengthens the church's pilgrimage toward trauma healing.

Most people of my age in South Sudan were born in war, studied in war, and were ordained to the ministry of God in war. Now we are still working and rendering our service in the context of violence and war. I want to believe that the Lord will call me to Himself in an atmosphere of peace. I want to believe that there is still a good morning or a day of sustainable and permanent peace for the people in South Sudan. But the trauma of the past violence and war surely hangs above our heads, minds, and hearts, impacting the normal lives of the people. All people in South Sudan are impacted by trauma. The "healers of healers" (church leaders, teachers, parents, and others) will require trauma healing. Youth and women will require it as well.

The harvest gathering of the Pilgrimage of Justice and Peace was organized by the WCC central committee and was held from 27 to 29 February 2020 at Lukenya Getaway, Kenya. Its main objective was to share experiences of the pilgrimage of justice and peace. The pilgrimage workshop identified two key needs: to increase trauma healing for the healers of healers and to increase the participation of youth and women in peacebuilding.

Practical Steps for Churches to Take

The church, by its very nature, is a peacemaker. It is what churches *are*, not just something that they *do*. Peace is more than just the absence of war, and the church commits to peacebuilding as a long-term process, even for decades: "Blessed are the peacemakers, for they will be called children of God" (Matt. 5:9).

It is out of its identity as peacemaker that the church in South Sudan must design a multi-ethnic and sectorial approach encompassing the following strategies:

- Continuous advocacy and engagement of the church to end the conflict

- Close work with parties to the conflict, ensuring that they devise mechanisms to resolve the conflict. Conflict resolution mechanisms should be set up at the local level.

- Indicators would include: 1) number of meetings, number of participants, and gender disaggregation; 2) community satisfaction, disaggregated by gender, age and group; 3) number of conflicts satisfactorily resolved; 4) decreased number of local conflicts.

- Communication, understanding, and restoration of relationships among communities and churches.

- Organization of dialogue platforms promoting dialogue and community reconciliation.

- Indicators would include: 1) Community satisfaction, disaggregated by group; 2) change of attitude of participants; 3) resolution of dialogue platforms; 3) increased role of women and youth in the platforms; 4) conflict/peace being monitored by platforms.

- Inculcation of a culture of forgiveness and reconciliation in communities through ecumenical sermons in different churches.

- Establishing well-designed and effective internal reconciliation mechanisms for church leaders.

- Strengthening SSCC and interreligious structures and capacities—technically and financially—as the moral beacon of South Sudan.

- Addressing conflict-related vulnerabilities and trauma-related shocks through trauma healing, reconciliation, and pastoral care.

- Providing trauma healing for the healers of healers. The church leaders are wounded healers who have been affected and injured by the pains and ravages of violence and war.

- Integration of peacebuilding interventions with food security and livelihood initiatives.

Toward an Inclusive Peacebuilding Process: Strengthening Social Cohesion in Syria

Michel Nseir

Development of the Programme

The 10th Assembly of the World Council of Churches (WCC) took place in Busan in October 2013, in a period when large areas of the Middle East and North Africa succumbed to violent sectarian, ethnic, and tribal animosities following popular uprisings in several countries. Reform movements that included hopes for political systems based on human rights and the rule of law were diverted by political radicalism and religious intolerance. The WCC member churches closely followed the development of the situation with a special concern and focus on continuous Christian presence and witness in the region and on the role of Christians, particularly youth, in maintaining the diversity in the region and in building democratic civil societies.

In the "Statement Affirming the Christian Presence and Witness in the Middle East," the assembly noted that "Christians today are aware that the guarantee of their free, engaged and meaningful existence in these societies is not by protection, nor a bequest given by political powers, but is acquired by forthright participation as citizens, and by persistent patience in encouraging mentalities and structures that enhance the free participation of all.... Christians in the region have contributed to the idea that plurality is a gift of God and that respect for diversity in plural societies is an affirmation that all peoples are created equal in the eyes of God."[1]

In this statement, the assembly theologically grounded the importance of the Christian presence and witness in the region, based on a policy statement of the central committee, meeting in Geneva in February 2011:

The WCC has viewed the Middle East as a region of special interest, being the birthplace of Judaism, Christianity, and Islam. . . . Our

---

1. "Statement Affirming the Christian Presence and Witness in the Middle East," *World Council of Churches 10th Assembly, 30 October–8 November 2013, Busan, Republic of Korea* (Geneva: WCC Publications, 2013), paras. 2.1, 2.2.

living faith has its roots in this land, and is nourished and nurtured by the unbroken witness of the local churches who have their own roots from the apostolic times. Without this Christian presence, the conviviality among peoples from different faiths, cultures, civilisations, which is a sign of God's love for all humanity, will be endangered. In addition, its extinction will be a sign of failure of the ecumenical family to express the Gospel imperative for costly solidarity.[2]

The statement also expressed the council's principles guiding its policy concerning the Middle East region: "God's justice and love for all of creation, the fundamental rights of all people, respect for human dignity, solidarity with the needy, and dialogue with people of other faiths." It finally noted that "political developments in the region point to signs of hope for democratic changes, respect for human rights and the rule of law in several countries."

The WCC programmatic work on Syria was undertaken in the context of the several WCC-initiated programmes and projects focusing on the Christian presence and witness in the Middle East, and under the framework of WCC statements and policy documents adopted by WCC governing bodies. In this context, the WCC facilitated a dialogue process between Syrians from diverse religious and ethnic backgrounds, linking it to the UN-facilitated peace process and the wider Geneva peace efforts. Five major high-level ecumenical consultations were held, involving the churches in Syria together with the wider ecumenical family:

- **9–10 December 2011: "Ecumenical Conversation on Emerging Trends in Syria,"** Geneva. Twenty church leaders from all confessional traditions in Syria came together to address their challenges and concerns and to envision their goals and expectations for the future of the Christian presence and witness in the region. Other church leaders from the wider ecumenical family also participated. Syrian Christians expressed their determination to find ways to be messengers of love and to convey the peace of God in Jesus Christ even amidst hostility and violence.

- **21–25 May 2013: International ecumenical conference on "Christian Presence and Witness in the Middle East,"** Notre-Dame du Mont Monastery, Lebanon. This meeting included

---

2. Minute on the Presence and Witness of Christians in the Middle East approved by the WCC Central Committee, meeting in Geneva 16-22 February 2011.

leaders and representatives from Christian churches in the Middle East, and churches and organizations from 34 other countries. It focused on strengthening the Christian presence and witness in the Middle East for the benefit of unity, justice, and peace for all in this region, in times of significant changes for the region and the world.[3]

- **18 September 2013: WCC Consultation on the Crisis in Syria, Geneva.** Church leaders from Syria, Russia, the United States, the United Kingdom, France, Germany, and Turkey, and representatives of international organizations in Geneva gathered together with Kofi Annan and the UN and Arab League Special Envoy for Syria, Lakhdar Brahimi. The joint communiqué made the following key points:

  - "Churches worldwide have spoken out against the war in Syria. Now is the time to raise one voice for peace and work for a negotiated solution to the conflict. . . . We must strengthen the public outcry so that those in power will protect the common interest of humanity."

  - "We believe there can be no military solution to the crisis in Syria. . . . Collective action for peace is needed to save not only the people of Syria but also the surrounding region as well."

  - "Christians in Syria are an integral part of a diverse society with a rich history. They have their place in civil society and commit themselves to build a future for Syria where citizens of all faiths enjoy equal rights, freedom and social justice. They are also committed to engage in constructive dialogues with other religious and ethnic communities so that Syria's pluralistic heritage is protected and secured."[4]

---

3. See the statement released by the conference: "Christian Presence and Witness in the Middle East," World Council of Churches and the Middle East Council of Churches International and Ecumenical Conference, 21–25 May 2013, Notre-Dame du Mont Monastery, Lebanon, https://www.oikoumene.org/resources/documents/statement-on-christian-presence-and-witness-in-the-middle-east.
4. "WCC Consultation on the Crisis in Syria, World Council of Churches communiqué," 18 September 2013, Geneva, https://www.oikoumene.org/resources/documents/communique-from-wcc-consultation-on-the-crisis-in-syria.

- **15–17 January 2014: WCC Ecumenical Consultation on Syria, Geneva.** This consultation issued the statement "An Urgent Call to Action for a Just Peace in Syria." Church leaders and representatives from Syria, the Middle East Council of Churches, the WCC, and the Holy See were present. They called for

  - Development of "a comprehensive and inclusive process toward establishing a just peace and rebuilding Syria. All sectors of society (including government, opposition, and civil society) need to be included in a Syrian solution for the Syrian people." Women and young people need to be fully integrated in these processes.

  - Preservation of "the multi-ethnic, multi-religious and multi-confessional nature and tradition of Syrian society . . . [with] equal rights for all of its citizens. Human rights, dignity and religious freedom for all must be promoted and protected in accordance with international norms."

  - Christians to speak "with one voice in calling for a just peace in Syria. To achieve this peace, we are committed to working hand-in-hand with Muslim sisters and brothers . . . seek[ing] to work for national reconciliation and healing through building trust."[5]

- **11–12 June 2014: Consultation at the Mother See of Holy Etchmiadzin, Armenia.**[6] At the invitation of His Holiness Karekin II Supreme Patriarch and Catholicos of all Armenians and in cooperation with the WCC, this consultation addressed the challenges for faith communities in the ongoing crisis in Syria. Church leaders and representatives from Syria, the Middle East Council of Churches, and the WCC took part.

---

5. "An Urgent Call to Action for a Just Peace in Syria," Statement for Geneva 2 talks on Syria, World Council of Churches, 17 January 2014, https://www.oikoumene.org/resources/documents/statement-for-geneva-2-talks-on-syria.
6. See "Communique from Church Leaders on Situation in Syria," Etchmiadzin, Armenai, 11–12 June 2014, https://www.oikoumene.org/resources/documents/communique-from-church-leaders-on-situation-in-syria

Principles for a Syrian Social Contract

Based on these conversations and the developments on the ground, the process described above evolved into a programme promoting peacebuilding and social cohesion through developing principles for a new social contract among Syrians based on a common narrative and vision for living together. This led, in late 2019, to the elaboration of 20 consensual principles summarized in a document entitled "Foundations for Living Together: Principles for a Syrian Social Contract."[7]

This programme, building on interfaith peace dialogue and the mobilization of local peace actors, is in line with WCC policies on Christian presence and witness in the Middle East adopted by its governing bodies since 2011, and policies on just peace adopted during the 10th assembly in Busan in 2013.

This programme is unique in its nature and purpose. In fact, there are several track 2 initiatives aiming at ending the conflict through mediating between some non-state armed groups and the Syrian government, facilitating conversation and dialogue between Syrian political actors, initiating discussions over future constitutional principles, addressing issues related to future security structures and governance, and developing economic plans. But in its programmatic work on Syria, the WCC is neither imitating nor duplicating those initiatives. In facilitating a genuine and credible dialogue among key religious and other civil society actors over issues that are essential for living together in mutual respect and equality, the WCC programme is regarded as unique in creating a paradigm shift in interreligious dialogue and cooperation that aims at developing a new social contract among different communities. This project attempts to address, in concrete ways, the real concerns of the different communities in order to reinforce social cohesion.

Aim and Objectives of the Programme

The aim of the programme is that social groups with different religious and ethnic identities work together to increase the level of social cohesion, strengthening the Syrian social fabric and national identity through a common quest for the best national model to manage diversity and devising patterns to enable the different communities to live together and contribute to building a democratic, diverse, inclusive, secure, stable, and unified Syria.

---

7. "Foundations for Living Together: Principles for a Syrian Social Contract," Center for Environmental and Social Development, 2019, https://www.etccmena.com/wp-content/uploads/Foundations-for-a-living-together_EN_Final_200130.pdf.

The main objectives:

- To develop and promote principles for living together in diversity in Syria, and to engage in a healing and recovery process through promoting social cohesion and preventing local tensions

- To engage a broad range of Syrian civil society and religious actors from different backgrounds in a dialogue for peace facilitated by the WCC, seeking the best national model to manage diversity, and devising patterns to enable the different communities to live together

- To strengthen the role and influence of women in the peace process and in society

Main Activities, Achievements, and Documents Produced

The project has directly reached more than 35,000 Syrians, in three tracks (Track 1: Decision makers; Track 2: Civil society main actors, including religious actors with direct reach to Track 1 actors; and Track 3: Grassroots level) through:

- Meetings in Geneva/Bossey

- Focus group discussions (FGDs)[8] from 2016 to present

- Survey on the "principles for a living together: towards a new social contract," that reached 9,600 Syrians

- Community Peace Groups in Syria, and different peacebuilding activities; and

- Building awareness sessions

The project has also produced a number of consensus documents:

- "Recommendation for a Syrian accord" (2015)[9]

- "Foundations for living together: Principles for a Syrian social contract" (2019)[10]

---

8. FGDs are inclusive groups of 15 to 18 participants each, where debates on principles for living together and other topics related to a new social contract in Syria are discussed.

9. Recommendation for a Syrian Accord, Center for Environmental and Social Development,

10. Foundations for Living Together: Principles for a Syrian Social Ccontract, Center for Environmental and Social Development, , https://www.etccmena.com/wp-content/uploads/Foundations-for-a-living-together_EN_Final_200130.pdf.

- Analytical report on the results of the survey

- Guidebook for the 20 principles

During the last 12 months, the following activities have been implemented:

- 3000 individual awareness sessions on the social contract definitions

- 62 focus group discussions (FGDs) in Syria; 34 in Turkey and Lebanon

- 18 awareness sessions on the rights for women as instituted by the Committee on the Elimination of All Forms of Discrimination against Women (CEDAW)[11] targeting women and men in the local community

- 55 media productions: video reports and products created by women media activists

- 34 peacebuilding meetings conducted by 7 local peace groups in 10 areas

- 30 day-long women's empowerment trainings on CEDAW topics and women's rights awareness

- 3 Geneva inter-religious meetings

- Peacebuilding activities designed and implemented by local CPGs to enhance social cohesion and civil peace and

- 60 day-long capacity-building trainings on topics such as journalism, video editing, and research

Conclusion: Lessons Learned

- Changes on the ground in Syria have resulted in the evolution of the programme, in terms of its activities, modalities, and forms of engagement. In the current context, closer engagement by WCC member churches of the region in the programme and its activities is essential.

- Inclusiveness and equal citizenship rights for the diversity of communities and identities in Syrian society is essential to ensure social cohesion and sustainable peace.

---

11. CEDAW is an international treaty adopted in 1979 by the UN GA. It is an international bill of rights for women and was instituted on 3 September 1981 and has been ratified by 189 states.

- In discussing issues related to their future and to the values that will enhance their living together, Syrians rediscover their common humanity.

- Concepts like *democracy, civil state, secularism,* and *separation between church and state,* should be relevant to the context in which they are to be used.

Messages from an Ecumenical Round Tables on Ukraine

Message from Round Table Held 30 March 2022
at the Bossey Ecumenical Institute, Switzerland

> *Steadfast love and faithfulness will meet; righteousness and peace will kiss each other.*
>
> *—Psalm 85:10*

The World Council of Churches (WCC) convened an ecumenical roundtable consultation on the situation in Ukraine, which took place on 30 March 2022 at the Bossey Ecumenical Institute, Switzerland. The following statement was produced at this consultation and endorsed by the signatories below.

At this time of war in Ukraine and widening divisions in the world, senior representatives of WCC member churches from several European countries neighbouring and directly affected by the current conflict gathered in Bossey, Switzerland, on 30 March 2022, upon the invitation of the Acting General Secretary of the World Council of Churches (WCC). The purpose of this meeting was to consult among us, to share perspectives on the conflict and its causes, and to discern possible paths forward for the churches together in working for peace in the midst of war. We regret that it was not possible for the representatives from Russia and Ukraine to travel to join us for this consultation, though they had accepted the invitation to do so.

We participants in this meeting collectively affirm—in line with the mandate and policy of the WCC—our rejection of war as against the will of God, and of the use of deadly military force as a means of resolving disputes—in Ukraine or anywhere else. Such disputes could and should be resolved peacefully, by sincere and meaningful dialogue and negotiations. We denounce the military aggression launched by the leadership of the Russian Federation against the people of the sovereign nation of Ukraine. We affirm the right of the people of Ukraine to defend themselves against this aggression. We grieve for all the precious lives already lost on both sides – each one of them so dear to God and to their loved ones—and for the terrible destruction and displacement of people and communities already caused.

We lift up the compassionate care and support offered to the Ukrainian refugees by the authorities, local communities, churches and church-related organizations in neighbouring and other countries, as a good example of the care and support all refugees fleeing from every such threat to life and dignity should receive.

We join in calling for a cease-fire in Ukraine, for humanitarian corridors to be opened and respected, and for sustained negotiations for a secure and just peace, to bring an end to this suffering.

We call urgently for recognition, respect and protection of the God-given human dignity of every human being in harm's way due to this or any other armed conflict, and appeal especially for the protection of all civilians and civilian infrastructure as a matter of fundamental moral duty, as well as a responsibility under international humanitarian law. All those responsible for violations of applicable laws and crimes against humanity must be held fully accountable for their actions.

Beyond the borders of Ukraine, and beyond the new diaspora of its displaced and suffering people, we are also gravely concerned about the even wider, longer-term consequences of this unjustifiable aggression. The global food security crisis, already acute as a result of the consequences of the COVID-19 pandemic, will now be vastly more severe, affecting especially the poorest and most vulnerable countries and communities of the world. Moreover, at this time when the whole world should be uniting in response to the common existential challenge of the looming climate catastrophe, the outrageous immorality of Russia's attack on its neighbour is greatly amplified.

We share the strong conviction that there is no legitimate way in which this armed aggression and its terrible consequences can be justified or tolerated from the perspective of our most fundamental Christian faith principles.

Acutely conscious of the grave risks of further escalation of the violence in Ukraine, of wider and even more destructive conflict, and of the abhorrent threat of weapons of mass destruction, we appeal for diplomacy instead of threats, dialogue instead of confrontation and exclusion, truth instead of disinformation, and for the voice of conscience—inspired by God's will for all the people of God and God's unique creation—to be heard.

As leaders of Christian communities facing this conflict and its consequences, and aware that sister churches hold different perspectives on the conflict's root causes, we stress the importance of the WCC as the ecumenical movement's leading instrument for sharing divergent perspectives, struggling with our differences, and seeking reconciliation and unity in word and deed to which our faith calls us. We join in fervent prayer for peace in Ukraine, in Europe and in the whole world, for the transformation of hearts and minds presently fixated on confrontation and violence, and for a turning to the path of peace where our Lord and Saviour Jesus Christ leads us.

We affirm the role of the WCC as a platform for ecumenical dialogue in the midst of such tragic conflict and political divisions, and the critical need for such dialogue—including with our counterparts from Russia and Ukraine—in this difficult context. We acknowledge the calling of churches and of the ecumenical movement to be peace-makers, and mutually commit to continuing to meet and to work together for justice and peace, counting on the good offices of the WCC to continue to convene us and enable our intent. We ask the WCC Acting General Secretary to renew his invitation to the WCC member churches in Russia and Ukraine to join us in another roundtable discussion as soon as possible.

Blessed are the peacemakers, for they will be called children of God.

—Matthew 5:9

H.E. Metropolitan Prof. Dr Nifon of Targoviste
Diocese of Targoviste (Romanian Orthodox Church)

Rt Rev. Dr Olav Fykse Tveit
Presiding Bishop, Church of Norway

Prälat Dr Martin Dutzmann
Evangelische Kirche in Deutschland

H.E. Archbishop Dr Vicken Aykazian
Diocese of the Armenian Apostolic Church

Archbishop Urmas Viilma
Estonian Evangelical Lutheran Church

Rev. Dr Kimmo Kääriäinen
Evangelical Lutheran Church of Finland

Mgr Ivan El'ko
General Bishop, Evangelical Church of the Augsburg Confession in Slovakia

Bishop Zoltán Balog
Ministerial President of the Synod, Reformed Church in Hungary

WCC staff:

Rev. Prof. Dr Ioan Sauca (convener)
Acting General Secretary

Marianne Ejdersten
Director, Communications

Peter Prove
Director, Commission of the Churches on International Affairs

Diana Chabloz
Assistant to the Acting General Secretary

Message from Round Table Held 10 June in Bossey, Switzerland

In a second ecumenical roundtable meeting convened by the World Council of Churches (WCC) on 10 June in Bossey, Switzerland, senior representatives of WCC member churches from several European countries neighbouring and directly affected by the current conflict gathered to consult each other on relevant developments since the first roundtable meeting held 30 March.

> He shall judge between many peoples,
>
> and shall arbitrate between strong nations far away;
>
> they shall beat their swords into ploughshares,
>
> and their spears into pruning-hooks;
>
> nation shall not lift up sword against nation,
>
> neither shall they learn war any more;
>
> but they shall all sit under their own vines and under their own fig trees,
>
> and no one shall make them afraid
>
> —*(Micah 4:3-4)*

Following the first ecumenical roundtable meeting on 30 March 2022, a second ecumenical roundtable meeting on the war in Ukraine was convened on 10 June 2022 in Bossey, Switzerland, upon the invitation of the acting general secretary of the World Council of Churches (WCC).

Senior representatives of WCC member churches from several European countries neighbouring and directly affected by the current conflict gathered to consult each other on relevant developments since the first roundtable meeting, and to discuss appropriate responses by the ecumenical movement, including in the context of the forthcoming WCC 11th Assembly in Karlsruhe, Germany, on 31 August-8 September 2022.

With very deep sadness and regret, we again missed the presence of representatives of the Russian Orthodox Church, due to very recent changes in the hierarchy of the Moscow Patriarchate, which had however been committed to taking part in our gathering. Obviously, the absence of these key counterparts constituted a fundamental obstacle to the purpose for which we convened – that of dialogue and mutual consultation.

We participants in this second meeting strongly reaffirm the joint ecumenical position expressed by the participants in the first roundtable meeting, especially the rejection of war as against the will of God, and of the use of deadly military force as a means of resolving disputes – in Ukraine or elsewhere. We reiterate our denunciation of the unjustified and illegal military aggression launched by the leadership of the Russian Federation against the people of the sovereign state of Ukraine. We call again for an immediate ceasefire and for dialogue and negotiations as the only morally acceptable path forward.

In addition to the terrible suffering of the people of Ukraine and the loss of precious lives on both sides, we also lift up again the consequences of this unjustifiable war for the poor and vulnerable of the entire world, especially due to the escalating global food crisis and the accelerating trajectory towards climate catastrophe driven by the effects of this conflict.

Despite the absence of our dialogue partners from Russia in this meeting, we re-emphasize the critical importance of the WCC as a platform for encounter and dialogue among the churches and communities most directly impacted by this war. This is the key and unique contribution that the global ecumenical movement can bring to the peaceful resolution of this crisis for which we all hope and pray. The calling to dialogue, encounter, and the pursuit of mutual understanding is the very essence of ecumenism. Division and exclusion is the antithesis of the purpose of our movement.

Nevertheless, we strongly reject the apparent instrumentalization of religious language by political and church leaders to support an armed invasion of a sovereign country. We cannot see this as anything other than fundamentally contradictory to our common understanding of core Christian and ecumenical principles. And for that reason, dialogue on the basis of truth and love is essential. It is urgently necessary to help turn the tide of division, confrontation, and conflict, and to help heal the deep wounds created in the global community by this brutal ongoing war.

We pray that the WCC 11thAssembly and its theme – Christ's love moves the world to reconciliation and unity – can provide both inspiration and momentum for the peace, reconciliation, and healing for which we yearn, and we ask the leadership of the WCC and its central committee to consider ways in which the assembly can most effectively serve this critical need.

Dr Agnes Abuom
World Council of Churches

Bishop Zoltán Balog
Reformed Church in Hungary

Bishop Dr Heinrich Bedford-Strohm
Evangelical Church in Germany

Archbishop Dr Antje Jackelén
Church of Sweden

Rev. Dr Kimmo Kääriäinen
Evangelical Lutheran Church of Finland

H.E. Archbishop of Prague and Czech Lands Michal
Orthodox Church in the Czech Lands and Slovakia

Bishop Peter Mihoc
Evangelical Church of the Augsburg Confession in Slovakia

Rev. Prof. Dr Ioan Sauca
World Council of Churches acting general secretary (convener)

H.E. Metropolitan Prof. Dr Nifon of Targoviste
Romanian Orthodox Church

Rt Rev. Dr Olav Fykse Tveit
Church of Norway

Archbishop Urmas Viilma
Estonian Evangelical Lutheran Church

Fr Jan Beranek
Orthodox Church in the Czech Lands and Slovakia (interpreter)

WCC staff

Marianne Ejdersten
Director Communication

Peter Prove
Director, Commission of the Churches on International Affairs

Diana Chabloz
Assistant to the Acting General Secretary

11

The World Council of Churches' Engagement for Just Peace in Colombia

Marcelo Schneider

The World Council of Churches has a long history of accompaniment and support for the churches and people of Colombia in their witness for justice and for peace during the long and brutal conflict in the country that has taken so many lives and disrupted and displaced so many families and communities. An attempt to establish an accompaniment programme—coordinated by the Latin American Council of Churches (CLAI) and supported by the World Council of Churches (WCC) and other actors, both locally and globally— was organized in 2009. This marks the starting point of the chronology of the WCC's direct involvement in the peace process in that country.

In December 2009, Colombia's attorney general reported 2,520 cases of forced disappearance out of 35,665 crimes confessed by the paramilitary forces. A reported 2388 pits were found in the country and 2,091 bodies exhumed, of which only 796 were returned to families. Guerrilla groups— FARC and ELN—also perpetrated massacres, indiscriminate attacks, evictions of farmers, torture, and sexual violence. In the department of Arauca alone, there were 194 homicides in 2009.

Columbian president Juan Manuel Santos has shown interest in meeting the humanitarian crisis regarding living victims of internal armed conflict. The government maintained an economic policy of opening the country to foreign investment. New armed groups—criminal gangs called "BaCrim", constituted chiefly by paramilitaries—started trying to control the territory and repel businesses linked to that policy.

The central aspect of the Programme of Ecumenical Accompaniment in Colombia (PEAC) was the option for non-violence, and it sought to support local and international efforts to achieve a negotiated solution to the conflict in Colombia. The programme supported the restitution of land to "displaced people," the defence of human rights, seeking justice and peace-building through dialogue, and it aims to encourage the presence of international ecumenical observers in specific areas for three months each.

The PEAC was launched during the first meeting of the expanded International Reference Group with church leaders in Colombia, which took place in Bogotá, Colombia, on 6-7 October 2009. In addition to CLAI and the WCC, the international ecumenical organizations which were involved included: ACT Alliance, World Communion of Reformed Churches, Lutheran World Federation, Regional Ecumenical Centre for Advocacy and Service (CREAS), KAIROS Canada and the National Council of the Churches of Christ in the USA.

The Programme's International Coordinator was Rev. Chris Ferguson of the United Church of Canada, a church with extensive ecumenical experience and one of the supporters of the Ecumenical Accompaniment Programme in Palestine and Israel (EAPPI), one of the models which inspired the initiative in Colombia.

The planning process of PEAC lasted from 2009 to 2012.

In 2012, while peace talks were already underway between the Colombian government and FARC rebels (Revolutionary Armed Forces of Colombia) in Norway, Dr Ricardo Esquivia of the Mennonite Church in Colombia affirmed that "creativity and audacity to advocate for justice in a nonviolent way" is essential now.

Speaking at the reference group of the PEAC in Bogota on 29 and 31 October 2012, he rejected the use of violence. "There are groups that get a lot of attention to their causes using violent ways. We reject that. We spread seeds of justice and want to cherish them as they grow," he said.

Esquivia, along with the Mennonite Church in Montes de Maria, was one of the founders of the PEAC. He defended that one of the challenges for the PEAC was to bring "development, advocacy and conflict resolution" together.

Also, by that time, Dr Marcelo Caruso, an academic, noted that dialogue between the Colombian government and the rebels was bringing the peace process to another level. Given the challenges in the peace process, he said, the PEAC programme would be able to receive its first ecumenical accompaniers soon. In other words, all conditions seemed favourable to start the implementation process.

A national coordinator for the PEAC was appointed: Blanca Echeverry. In her first public statement as national coordinator, she said: "We want to help strengthen and build the capacity of organizations and communities in the affected areas in Colombia, strengthening their social participation and organization." PEAC aims to advocate for people's "economic, social, political, cultural, environmental and territorial rights."

On 31 October 2012, members of PEAC's international reference group travelled to the region of Montes de María and met with local authorities and communities. The town of San Onofre was chosen to be the first to receive accompaniers by December 2012.

The start-up of PEAC

The programme's structure and specific roles were defined:

a. A **National Reference Group** (NRG) is responsible for orientation, monitoring and evaluation of the programme and for selecting a national coordinator and a staff person for communications. This group comprised members of the CLAI Colombia Roundtable, the CLAI general secretary, a representative of the ACT Colombia Forum, a representative of the Inter-Ecclesiastical Justice and Peace Commission, and one representative from each of the accompanied communities. Other organisations involved in accompaniment may be added to this group. The National Reference Group Colombia was meant to deal with decisions around programming and programme priorities. The Colombian Methodist Church (IMC) was entrusted with administering the PEAC finances.

b. The **International Reference Group** (IRG) is responsible for supporting the functions of the international coordinator and the National Reference Group through fund-raising, development of the programme, and awareness-raising both about the program and the communities being accompanied. It should develop strategic alliances, provide guidance for formulating advocacy policies, and support all advocacy initiatives. The IRG is made up of representatives of the World Council of Churches, ACT Alliance, World Communion of Reformed Churches, the Lutheran World Federation (LWF), the Latin American Council of Churches (CLAI), the Regional Ecumenical Advisory and Service Centre (CREAS), and sister organizations like KAIROS Canada, Church World Service. The CLAI secretary general convened the IRG.

The proposal anticipated the implementation of the project in three phases:

Phase One - 2012: implementation of the project, including a pilot project in one of the zones.

Phase Two - 2013-2015: further implementation, PEAC operational in five zones. Complete development of the advocacy and communications strategies.

Phase Three - 2016: full implementation in seven zones. Evaluation of PEAC.[1]

At this stage, the role of the WCC was mainly focused on giving present and future visibility to PEAC through communications. In November 2012, a member of the WCC communications team travelled with a videographer to the region of San Onofre to document the work of the first group of accompaniers and produce a video of PEAC.

A pilot experience & a rapid demise

In 2012, the international coordinator travelled and entertained meetings with churches and ecumenical organizations in different countries, seeking support for the EAPC and hoping to establish national co-ordinations. The first group of Ecumenical Accompaniers in 2013 came from the Student Christian Movements in Mexico and the Dominican Republic. The World Student Christian Federation (WSCF) adopted the PEAC as a global priority, and the WSCF Latin American region was eager to participate.

That first group was placed in the communities of San Onofre and Finca La Alemania in the Sucre Department, northern Colombia.

At some point in 2012, discrepancies began building up between the international coordinator and some heads of churches concerning the orientation and overall functioning of the program. Those tensions further developed between the appointed local coordinator, Blanca Echeverry, and the international coordinator. The discord came to a climax during the assembly of CLAI in Havana (May 2013), where a meeting of representatives from Colombian churches, United Church of Canada, WCC, ACT and other regional and international ecumenical bodies was held to appraise the evolution of the PEAC.

There were several meetings of the National Reference Group and the International Reference Group via Skype in 2013. A meeting involving locals and internationals was held in Bogota in June 2013 to evaluate the first

---

1. The budgets amounted to $199 288 (2012) and $159 038 (2013).

outcomes of the project and seek solutions to pending issues. Yet, after the Havana meeting, it was clear that the PEAC had already begun its definitive decline.

At the June 2013 meeting, Lutheran Bishop Eduardo Martínez was asked to provide pastoral care to the national and international coordinators, given the serious deterioration of their relationship. A decision to carry out an evaluation of the PEAC was also taken at that meeting.

The findings and recommendations of the evaluation were discussed at a meeting held in August 2013. One of the findings was very significant: "The attitude of various bishops difficult and limit the functioning of the program. . . . What keeps hindering PEAC is that attitude focusing on power and control. The program should have a more horizontal, democratic structure."

Despite ongoing structural and relational problems, Colombian church leaders and representatives from ecumenical organizations who met in Bogota that August issued a statement confirming their commitment and willingness to continue and strengthen the Ecumenical Accompaniment Programme in Colombia. "Our reaffirmation of the EAPC responds to the humanitarian crisis and human rights violation affecting the country, manifested in all its crudity in the regions where we are present, affecting the lives of people and jeopardizing the guarantees of rights Community leaders and human rights defenders," reads their statement.

Nonetheless, the PEAC would cease to function in the following months, a decision by the heads of churches despite their affirmation of the program.

One of the issues with the PEAC was the distancing from ecumenical bodies and civil society organizations with a meaningful history of peace and justice work in the country. From the onset, some heads of churches claimed complete ownership of the program and tried to control it.

But most significant recent endeavours in Colombia around peace and justice issues usually involve a few churches and a significant number of ecumenical, para-ecclesial, and civil society organizations.

Thus, for instance, the Ecumenical Peace Table (Mesa Ecuménica por la Paz), created in 2011/2012, is formed mainly by grassroots groups and individuals with an ecumenical commitment who wish to contribute to the peace process and the current peace dialogues from their Christian identity.[2]

In this context, another initiative called DiPaz (Inter-ecclesial Dialogue for Peace) was launched by Mennonites, Presbyterians, Lutherans, and Roman Catholics. The five Protestant churches involved in the PEAC, which are also members of CLAI (Anglican, Lutheran, Presbyterian, Methodist and Mennonite), had different understanding and stances vis-à-vis the 60-year civil war in the country.

For many years, the Mennonite Church has taken up initiatives to build bridges between warring factions. They are very clear that it is the church's vocation and mandate to dialogue with any armed group willing to do so in the search for peace for Colombia.

Since its establishment in 1990, the Mennonite's Christian Centre for Justice, Peace, and Nonviolent Action (Justapaz) has worked to promote nonviolence, peace-building, and the positive transformation of conflict. It has developed a broad range of training, organization, and action initiatives for conflict transformation at local, regional, national, and international levels.

The Presbyterian Church has a record of human rights work supporting Colombians internally displaced by the violence. The Presbyterian Peace Fellowship, PC(USA) World Mission and the Presbyterian Church of Colombia have worked together in training and deploying short-term mission workers to Colombia over the years.

With the support of the Lutheran World Relief, the Lutheran Church has been helping victims of violence find empowerment in rebuilding their lives, building income, getting involved in civics and gaining influence in their communities.

The different attitudes ostensibly sprung out of political, theological, and institutional considerations.

---

2. This body organized the International Ecumenical Encounter for Peace in Colombia in April 2015, attended by over 300 people. It was supported by the World Council of Churches, ACT Alliance, the World Communion of Reformed Churches, the Mennonite World Congress Foundation, Danish Church Aid , Lutheran World Federation Department for World Service, CLAI , World Vision, United Methodist Church Global Ministries, Disciples and Church of Christ USA, and the Lutheran Church of Norway among other. The Roman Catholic Church was represented through its Inter-ecclesial Commission of Justice and Peace.

The WCC working closely with the Colombian government and DiPAZ

With the appointment of Mr Rudelmar Bueno de Faria as the Ecumenical United Nations Office (EUNO) coordinator in New York in 2013, the engagement of the WCC with the peace process in Colombia changed from a more punctual approach to a more strategic system of cooperation.

In March 2015, the EUNO attended the WCSF Assembly in Bogota, Colombia, and facilitated a discussion on peace and security. In this opportunity, the WCC EUNO met with civil society organizations and the ambassador from Norway to learn more about the perspectives of the peace agreements.

In July 2015, the EUNO organized an Ecumenical Conversation on Colombia in New York with Ms Jenny Neme, Director of the Mennonite Association for Justice, Peace, and Do No Harm—JUSTAPAZ on Peace Process in Colombia—Enabling Peace, Justice, and Reconciliation. NGOs, the UN and ecumenical organizations attended the event.

The EUNO coordinator joined the WCC delegation visiting Colombia (7-9 September 2015) in the context of the Pilgrimage of Justice and Peace. A meeting with President Juan Manuel Santos took place at the presidential palace on 7 September and with the Minister of Interior the same day.

The EUNO coordinator stayed an additional day to maintain conversations with the Minister of the Interior's Office for Religious Affairs and explore joint actions to promote a just and lasting peace in Colombia. The WCC general secretary headed the delegation undertaking the Pilgrimage of Justice and Peace through Latin America, which ended in Colombia.

On 6 September 2015, an inter-religious meeting organized by a WCC member (Presbyterian Church) in Colombia took place, with approximately 30 representatives of church leaders (bishops and presidents) from different denominations, Islamic and Jewish leaders, and interfaith and ecumenical organizations. The discussions were around the Pilgrimage of Justice and Peace, as well as an exchange of ideas on how to address issues related to the peace process in Colombia. The meeting affirmed WCC as an important actor in supporting the ecumenical movement in the post-conflict situation.

After the meeting, the WCC delegation participated in an ecumenical service organized by the Presbyterian Church of Colombia. Rev. Tveit led the sermon and, after the service, gave an interview for a local TV station on the purpose of the visit to Colombia, as well as the WCC Pilgrimage of Justice and Peace. A lunch with pastors and representatives from the Bogota Synod of the Presbyterian Church also took place.

In the afternoon, the delegation met with representatives of DIPAZ (Inter-Church Dialogue for Peace) and ACT Alliance on the Lutheran World Federation (LWF) premises.

Representatives from the Catholic Church, Presbyterian Church, Lutheran Church, Church of Sweden, LWF, LWR, Christian Aid, CREAS, and CLAI were in the meeting. The group delivered a letter to the WCC general secretary highlighting the utmost importance thereof that the international religious and faith-based community publicly demonstrates its support for the legitimate work of minority religions and non-Catholic churches in Colombia, such as the efforts made by DIPAZ. The letter also asked for three major actions from the general secretary:

- Monitor and follow up on the government's commitment to developing a policy on religious freedom

- Contribute to strengthening participation by non-Catholic religious actors in the peace process, especially in the Truth Commission

- Consider assembling a delegation of Colombian and international religious leaders to travel to Havana, Cuba, to meet with the peace negotiators.

On the evening of that day, the general secretary met with the Norwegian ambassador. Rev. Gloria Ulloa, the WCC regional president for Latin America and the Caribbean, together with two WCC staff members, met with Ms Lilia Solano, a politician engaged in the peace process in connection with the negotiators in La Habana. She provided relevant information on the peace process, highlighting that an agreement is expected to be reached by January or February of the next year. She also urged WCC to take a role in the post-agreement by supporting churches to play a meaningful role in reconciliation and reconstruction activities, including the Truth Commission. CREAS and CLAI also participated in this meeting.

The WCC delegation attended a meeting organized by the Coordinator of Religious Affairs of the Ministry of Interior, Lorena Ríos, with the representatives of the Episcopal Conference and the Presbyterian Church of Colombia, Anglican, Greek Orthodox, Seventh Day Adventist, United

Pentecostal, Christian Methodist, Mennonite, Lutheran, Baptist, Colombia Assemblies of God, Latin American Council of Churches, CONFERILEC, CEDECOL, Lutheran World Federation, Reconciliation Colombia, JUSTAPAZ, Baptist University, Teusaquillo Territory of Peace, and CREAS.

The WCC General Secretary used the Pilgrimage of Justice and Peace to call religious leaders to engage in the peace process in Colombia. The religious leaders expressed satisfaction with the engagement of WCC in supporting the peace process in the country.

After the discussions with the religious leaders, the Minister of Interior, Mr Juan Fernando Cristo, joined the meeting. Rev. Olav Fykse Tveit expressed WCC's support of the post-conflict process. He said that it is the nature of the church to assist on issues such as reconciliation, forgiveness, and repentance. He said that churches in Colombia also have the support of the international community, highlighted by the diversity of faith-based organizations and their work to achieve just peace. After the meeting, the minister and Rev. Tveit gave a press conference.

The minister, Juan Fernando Cristo, thanked WCC for the support and reiterated that "the role of these churches is essential in the region." He appreciated this collective effort to build a climate of peace after signing the agreement in Havana.

The delegation had an audience with Colombian President Juan Manuel Santos at the presidential palace, Casa de Nariño, in Bogota to discuss the peace process in Colombia. During the meeting with President Juan Manuel Santos, Rev. Tveit shared information about the direct participation of the WCC in different peace processes around the world and the willingness of the local and global ecumenical fellowship to be part of the implementation of the peace process after the agreement is signed. He said that "the churches believe in reconciliation, forgiveness and repentance, and are committed to contribute to the peace-building process."

He added that "churches in Colombia have the full support of the ecumenical international community" in their pursuit of peace in their country. President Santos expressed his interest in having the international community, represented by the WCC and its member churches in the region, contribute to building justice and peace in the country in the post-conflict situation.

The delegation visited the Latin American Episcopal Council of the Roman Catholic Church (CELAM). Monsignor Juan Espinoza, general secretary of CELAM, recalled the commitment of the church to justice and peace and shared the commitment of CELAM and the Latin American churches to promote peace in the world today.

On 8 September 2015, two WCC staff members attended an event organized by DIPAZ called "Discerning the Peace Process in Colombia." This meeting brought together about 40 people from different ecumenical organizations and churches, including CLAI. Three external resource persons were invited to make a presentation on the current situation in Colombia. The WCC representative was invited to share the outcomes from the WCC delegation visit to Colombia, as well as the actions WCC may take to support the peace process in the country.

As an outcome of those discussions, WCC was requested to facilitate a workshop on 3-4 November 2015 in Bogota for Dipaz and ACT Alliance members. The workshop was intended to draw a clear advocacy plan for Diaz and ACT Alliance.

On 9 September 2015, the EUNO coordinator met with Ms Lorena Rios from the office of the Minister of Interior. She requested support from WCC to bring religious leaders together to engage in reconciliation and reconstruction. More specifically, she asked WCC to help her department find international support for a project called "Formulation of Public Policy for Religious Freedom and Belief." She also asked if WCC could support two advisors for her office to build up these public policies.

Key follow-up issues from that strategic visit in 2015 were:

- Monitor and follow up on the government's commitment to developing a policy on religious freedom

- Contribute to strengthening participation by non-Catholic religious actors in the peace process, especially in the Truth Commission

- Consider assembling a delegation comprised of Colombian and International religious leaders to travel to Havana, Cuba, to meet with the peace negotiators

- Facilitate a workshop on advocacy for peace on 3-4 November 2015 in Bogota for members of Dipaz and ACT Alliance

- To explore with possible donor agencies funding for a project for "Formulation of Public Policy for Religious Freedom and Belief" to be carried out in cooperation with WCC and the Minister of Interior

- To meet with the Minister of Interior - Secretary for Religious Affairs in November 2015 to follow up discussions of the general secretary's visit

- Consult Fr Michael Lapsley about his availability to travel to Colombia to be on a panel on reconciliation

At this point, the internal reflections between EUNO and Geneva pointed to a need to reflect on the best way to support the peace process in Colombia. It would require a clear definition of responsibilities between Geneva, New York, and Porto Alegre (where a key WCC staff member was based) to consider becoming involved in the peace talks between the Colombian government and the ELN.

On 3 and 4 November 2015, the EUNO sponsored, in cooperation with the LWF, a workshop on advocacy for peace in Colombia. Participants of the ACT Alliance local forum and DIPAZ (Inter-ecclesial Dialogue for Peace) produced an action plan for peace in Colombia.

On 5 November, the EUNO was invited to be the key speaker at an International Conference on Faith-based Communities and Organizations: Promoters of Peace. The Religious Affairs Office of the Minister of Interior of Colombia organised the event. This event was a follow-up to the discussion held by the WCC delegation with the Colombian government in September 2015.

In 2016, the Colombian Ministry of Interior, Office for Religious Affairs, requested support from WCC to support and facilitate 32 departmental meetings as of June 2016 to carry out actions to strengthen the religious sector. They would discuss elaborating a national policy for religious bodies in each territory. The WCC Vice President for Latin America was one of the two sponsored participants provided by WCC. They would travel to the departments and intervene in these meetings, explaining the perspective of the religious sector in peace-building and the potential contribution of religious leaders in post-conflict and reconciliation.

At that time—considering the decision of the UN Security Council to establish a political mission of unarmed international observers responsible for monitoring and verification of the laying down of arms and the tripartite mechanism that would monitor and verify the definitive bilateral ceasefire and cessation of hostilities following the signing of the Final Peace Agreement between the Government of Colombia and the FARC-EP—civil society organizations and churches were concerned with the narrow perspective of the mission.

DIPAZ requested WCC to facilitate a visit of a delegation to New York to meet with members of the United Nations Security Council on the agenda related to the peace process talks between the Colombian Government, FARC-EP and ELN, and in particular on bilateral ceasefire and hostilities; unarmed protection of communities; interventions in the Truth Justice System Repair and guarantees of non-Repetition role in the early recognition of responsibility; and proposed reforms under the point of democracy for peace and end the armed conflict.

WCC facilitated these meetings in July 2016.

EUNO was invited to participate in an international conference organized by the Government of Colombia on 5 and 6 July 2016 in Bogota. The participants were mainly interreligious leaders and also governmental agencies and the UN.

In September 2015, the WCC general secretary issued a statement on the historic announcement made by the Colombian government and the FARC rebels agreeing to end 50 years of internal conflict and working towards addressing issues of justice and reparations to the victims.

"This peace deal in Colombia is vital a sign of hope not only for Colombians but also for the whole world. We congratulate both leaders for their announced commitment to clear the path for a final peace agreement to be signed within the next months," he wrote.

He also stressed that "Churches in Colombia, along with civil society, have been striving for justice and peace since several decades. An end to the conflict promises a new dawn of stability for the Colombian people."

The EUNO has closely accompanied the peace process in Colombia. Visits were undertaken to Bogota to meet with churches, FBOs and government authorities, and delegations from Colombia were received in New York for advocacy work and public events. Some activities related to the EUNO engagement are described in the program section.

On 18 April 2016, EUNO and Caritas Internationalis organized a hearing with representatives from Colombian civil society on the peace process in the country. Cristina Espanel and Marco Romero, human rights defenders, were among the speakers.

EUNO was one of the co-organizers of the WCC international consultation on "Peace building and Reconciliation: The Place of the Church", which took place 8-11 June in Soweto, South Africa, to commemorate where black children revolted against inferior apartheid education in 1976.

The consultation gathered 55 participants from Burundi, Colombia, the Democratic Republic of Congo, Nigeria, Palestine, South Africa, South Sudan, and Sudan, as well as representatives from the SACC, specialized ministries, WCC commission members, and WCC leadership and staff.

On 4 July, EUNO attended a meeting at the presidential palace in Bogota, where Colombian President Juan Manuel Santos signed the decree establishing the National Day of Religious Freedom and Worship. The ceremony gathered more than 100 religious leaders, including Roman Catholics, Protestants, Jews, Muslims, and representatives of international organizations such as the WCC. The EUNO coordinator spoke on behalf of the WCC at the request of the President.

The EUNO coordinator was also the keynote speaker during the International Conference on Peace, which took place from 05-06 July in Bogota, Colombia, organized by the Ministry of Interior of Colombia. More than 600 religious leaders, government officials, and politicians attended the conference.

From 15-19 August, EUNO organized and hosted the visit of a delegation from the churches in Colombia to New York. The delegation met with eight ambassadors of the UN Security Council and participated in an event organized by EUNO and Caritas Internationalis called "Building a Just and Sustainable Peace Process in Colombia."

In May 2017, already as part of the dialogue process between the Colombian government and ELN *(Ejército de la Liberacion Nacional)* taking place in Quito, Ecuador, the WCC CCIA received an invitation to engage in the first phase of dialogue with ELN representatives. A delegation of 3 WCC representatives were to meet the ELN dialogue delegation, in Quito, on 7 June 2017.

The pilgrimage of justice and peace focus

The WCC took various initiatives in 2018 to focus on the situation in Colombia and to re-emphasize the importance of international ecumenical support for realizing the hopes of the people of Colombia for justice and peace. In particular, several Pilgrim Team Visits were undertaken to different parts of the country. The Reference Group of the Pilgrimage of Justice and Peace and the Theological Study Group met in Bogota, Colombia. Pilgrim Team Visits (PTVs) went to Apartadó, Curaradó, and Chocó, Cali and Cauca, Valledupar, Barranquilla, and Cartagena in Colombia. The Commission of the Churches on International Affairs (CCIA) also had its 55th meeting in Cartagena, and the public forum organized by CCIA on 28 February 2018 on "The Peace Process in Colombia, and the role of churches and faith communities" with HE Juan Manuel Santos, President of the Republic of Colombia and 2016 Nobel Peace Prize laureate, as a key speaker. At the public forum, Rev. Frank Chikane, the moderator of the WCC Commission on International Affairs, explained to the President of Colombia that the CCIA meeting in Colombia is meant to discern what the WCC could do to help address the challenges faced by the people of Colombia and to support and encourage the hopes for peace. It follows a long history of ecumenical efforts to accompany the search for peace in Colombia and to support the WCC's member church—the Presbyterian Church of Colombia—and the other churches and faith communities of Colombia in working for peace, justice, and human dignity.

He emphasised that the calling of every church and every Christian is to recognize the image of God in every human being and be peacemakers among those in conflict. He also shared with the president about the CCIA visits to various communities to listen and understand the challenges they face and what they think needs to be done to have lasting peace and justice for all. He said, "As a South African, I can see similarities between our experience and what you are going through, and I believe we can help each other to cross this bridge. I want to appreciate the engagement and leadership of President Santos in the pursuit of peace in this country, recognized in the award of the 2016 Nobel Peace Prize. And we welcome this opportunity to engage in a dialogue on the status of the peace process and the role of churches and faith communities."

The speech of Prof. Dr Isabel Apawo Phiri, WCC deputy general secretary, to the president raised the concerns of Afro-Colombian, Indigenous and other rural communities, as well as demobilized FARC members and government officials who were visited during the PTVs. She said: "From what we have heard and seen, we are concerned that the future of the peace process you have led, and to which we are committed, is in jeopardy. We have heard a great deal of disillusionment and frustration regarding the slow and partial implementation of the government commitments under the accord with the FARC. To restore confidence in the possibility of peace, we believe that full implementation of all the commitments made under the peace accord is of critical importance. It is also important that both the ELN and the government refrain from renewed violence, return to the negotiating table, and establish a new ceasefire until an agreement can be reached. And it is very important that those who seek to promote and protect human rights, to represent civil society, simply to provide leadership for their communities, are protected from violence and harassment. We want to believe that no one in this country desires the continuation of conflict but that all share the aspiration and need for peace, justice, and dignity. These are the values that we in the World Council of Churches wish to work with the churches, faith communities, civil society, and government authorities of Colombia to secure for all people in this country."

These concerns were reflected in the public statement on building just peace in Colombia of the central committee of June 2018.

Unfortunately, with the change of government in Colombia, the peace process in Colombia has taken a different direction.

Afterword—Our Feet into the Way of Peace

Since the 10th Assembly of the World Council of Churches in Busan in 2013, the ecumenical efforts for peacebuilding and reconciliation have been a key programme emphasis for the fellowship of the WCC. The 2014 WCC central committee approved a document that gave more flesh to the Pilgrimage of Justice and Peace, focusing on the theme of peacebuilding in certain conflict countries. The priority countries designated for immediate international accompaniment included the Democratic Republic of Congo, Israel and Palestine, Nigeria, the Korean Peninsula, South Sudan, Syria, and Ukraine. Since then, the number of priority countries has increased to include Iraq, Burundi, and Colombia.

This book contains reflections and lessons learned from churches' ecumenical engagement for peacebuilding since the 10th assembly in these countries. The title of the book, *Our Feet into the Way of Peace,* indeed represents churches' ecumenical efforts for peace as a way of living in fellowship with God, as expressed in Zechariah's prayer:

> By the tender mercy of our God,
>
> the dawn from on high will break upon us,
>
> to give light to those who sit in darkness and in the shadow of death,
>
> to guide *our feet into the way of peace"*
>
> (Luke 1:78–79, emphasis added)

Contributors to this publication provided inspiring information on strengthening the ecumenical bonds for peacebuilding. This information is essential background for understanding the critical and urgent necessity of ending war, internal conflict, and division, and for building a sustainable peace regime in these priority countries.

This publication will be a background resource for Ecumenical Conversation 14, the Ecumenical Call to Just Peace: Holistic Approaches to Peacebuilding, at the WCC's 11th Assembly in Karlsruhe. The ecumenical conversation will seek to identify best practices and lessons learned from the experiences of churches in the peace process in priority countries and to further develop the ecumenical approach to holistic peacebuilding.

We hope that through this publication, you may be encouraged and empowered to amplify and strengthen holistic approaches to peacebuilding, and to join in renewing hope for peace in these priority countries.

Ibrahim Wushishi Yusuf
Jin Yang Kim

Contributors

Rev. Dr Jin Yang Kim is a member of clergy of the Northern Illinois Annual Conference of the United Methodist Church and the coordinator of the Pilgrimage of Justice and Peace at the World Council of Churches in Geneva.

Michel Nseir has been working with the World Council of Churches since September 2007 on programmes focusing on the Middle East and has developed a deep understanding of the cultural, political, and religious dynamics prevalent in the region. Before joining the WCC, he lectured at the St John of Damascus Institute of Theology at the University of Balamand and other schools of theology in Lebanon from 1996 to 2007. He served as executive secretary of the Association of Theological Seminaries and Institutes in the Middle East from 1998 to 2004. He holds a master's degree in Orthodox theology from Balamand and a High Diploma in Biblical Studies from the Catholic Institute in Paris.

The Most Reverend Bernard Ntahoturi was born in Matana, Burundi, and trained for the Anglican ordained ministry in the Bishop Tucker School of Divinity and Theology–Uganda Christian University. He was consecrated Bishop in 1998 and became Archbishop of the Anglican Church of Burundi in 2005 until his retirement in 2016. He served on the WCC central committee from the time of the assembly in Harare (1998) to the assembly in Busan (2013). He co-chaired the first Permanent Committee on Consensus and Collaboration. He worked actively in strengthening the ecumenical humanitarian agency Act Alliance. He represented the Burundi National Council of Churches as an observer in the Burundi Peace and Reconciliation negotiations held in Arusha, Tanzania. He was the vice-chair of the first Burundi Truth and Reconciliation Commission.

Celine Osukwu is a recipient of a WCC scholarship. As a leader in development issues and an advocate of inclusion, she has served in various ecumenical movements. She is the Nigerian contact person for the Ecumenical Disability Advocates Network and a member of the International Reference Group, Ecumenical Advocacy Alliance of WCC.

Fr. James Oyet Latansio is a Catholic priest and General Secretary of the South Sudan Council of Churches (SSCC), where he has provided leadership since April 2015. Having grown up through decades of war, Fr. James is passionate about peace and reconciliation. As SSCC General Secretary, he works in partnership with the SSCC Core Group that includes ACT Alliance members, the CARITAS group, and KAIROS Canada, particularly in initiatives to enhance peacebuilding, healing, and reconciliation in South Sudan. The SSCC plays a critical role in building sustainable peace through implementing its Action Plan for Peace.

Rev. Ibrahim Wushishi Yusuf is an ordained pastor in the Nigerian Baptist Convention. He received pastoral training at the Baptist Theological Seminary, Faith Christian Theological Seminary Lagos, and the Nigerian Defence Academy. He has served in pastoral ministry and peace and interfaith work in Nigeria for many years and served in various leadership positions within and outside the Baptist denomination, including as general secretary of the Christian Council of Nigeria, co-secretary of the International Centre for Interfaith Peace and Harmony, and member of the Nigeria Interreligious Council. He is currently the programme executive for Peacebuilding in the African Region at the World Council of Churches.

Rev. Seung-Min Shin is the director of international relations at the National Council of Churches in Korea. He was the executive secretary for ecumenical relations of the Presbyterian Church in the Republic of Korea. He was also the regional secretary of the World Student Christian Federation Asia-Pacific.

Rev. Ephraim Yakubu Simon is a director of the Christian Council of Nigeria and an adjunct lecturer at Baptist College of Theology, Jos, Nigeria. He is a member of the Institute of Professional Managers and Administrators of Nigeria and an alumnus of Kofi Annan International Peace Training Centre in Accra, Ghana. He has attended courses on conflict transformation within and outside Nigeria. He is a doctoral candidate in pastoral care and pastoral ministry at the Faculty of Theological Studies, Nigerian Baptist Theological Seminary Ogbomoso, Nigeria.

Prof. Rev. Dr Paul Mpongo Tshihamba is President of the Ecumenical Forum of Member Churches and the All Africa Conference of Churches in the Democratic Republic of Congo. He is the Alternate Legal Representative of the ECC/31st Presbyterian Community in Congo 31st CPC Kinshasa, DRC. He is a professor of Systematic Theology and Academic General Secretary

Fr Emanuel Youkhana is ordained as Archimandrite for the Assyrian Church of the East. He is now the secretary of the Literature Committee of the Assyrian Church of the East. He served as Iraqi Kurdistan Coordinator for the International Society for Human Rights and was awarded the Stephanus Stiftung prize for work on behalf of the persecuted. .

Bishop Dr Munib A. Younan is the former president of the Lutheran World Federation and former bishop of the Evangelical Lutheran Church in Jerusalem and the Holy Land. He was a member of the Board of Trustees of Al Diyar Consortium in Bethlehem. He worked to coordinate the Committee for Cooperation between the ELCJHL and overseas partners.

Prof. Dr Isabel Apawo Phiri is Deputy General Secretary: Public Witness and Diakonia of the World Council of Churches. She received her Bachelor of Education from the University of Malawi and holds a master's degree in Religious Education from the University of Lancaster, England, and a Doctorate in Religious Studies from the University of Cape Town, South Africa. She was previously a professor of African theology, Dean and Head of the School of Religion, Philosophy and Classics at the University of KwaZulu Natal in South Africa and also served as general coordinator of the Circle of Concerned African Women Theologians and was on the International Reference Group of EHAIA. She served on the Bossey Board and was moderator of the Commission on Ecumenical Education and Formation of the WCC.

WCC Publications 2018-2022

A comprehensive list of WCC Publications can be found https://www.oikoumene.org/resources/publications

Donald Norwood, *Pilgrimage of Faith: The Journey of the WCC,* 2018, ISBN: 978-2-8254-1710-2

Carlos Sentado and Manuel Quintero Perez, *A Legacy of Passionate Ecumenism,* 2018, ISBN: 978-2-8254-1711-9

Susan Durber and Fernando Enns, eds., *Walking Together: Reflections on the Ecumenical Pilgrimage of Justice and Peace,* 2018, ISBN: 978-2-8254-1712-6

J. Michael West and Gunnar Mägi, eds., *Your Word Is Truth: The Bible in Ten Christian Traditions,* 2018, ISBN: 978-2-8254-1714-0

J. Michael West and Gunnar Mägi, eds., *Your Word Is Truth: The Bible in Ten Christian Traditions,* eBook edition, 2018, ISBN: 978-2-8254-1715-7

Treatment Adherence and Faith Healing in the Context of HIV and AIDS in Africa (EHAIA), 2018, ISBN: 978-2-8254-1716-4

Treatment Adherence and Faith Healing in the Context of HIV and AIDS in Africa (EHAIA), Kiswahili edition, 2018, ISBN: 978-2-8254-1717-1

Treatment Adherence and Faith Healing in the Context of HIV and AIDS in Africa (EHAIA), French edition, 2018, ISBN: 978-2-8254-1718-8

Positive Masculinities and Femininities: Handbook for Adolescents and Young People in Faith Communities in Nigeria, English edition, 2018, ISBN: 978-2-8254-1719-5

Translating the Word, Transforming the World: An Ecumenical Reader, 2018, ISBN: 978-2-8254-1712-6

Amélé Adamavi-Aho Ekué, Pamela D. Couture, and Samuel George, eds., *For Those Who Wish to Dream: Emerging Theologians on Mission and Evangelism,* 2019, ISBN: 978-2-8254-1724-9

Risto Jukko and Jooseop Keum, eds. *Moving in the Spirit: Report of the WCC Conference on World Mission and Evangelism,* 2019, ISBN: 978-2-8254-1721-8

Risto Jukko (Ed.), *Moving in the Spirit: Report of the WCC Conference on World Mission and Evangelism,* Complete Digital Edition, 2019, ISBN: 978-2-8254-1722-5

Risto Jukko, Jooseop Keum, and (Kay) Kyeong-Ah Woo, eds., *Called to Transforming Discipleship: Devotions from the WCC Conference on World Mission and Evangelism,* 2019, ISBN: 978-2-8254-1723-2

Come and See: A Theological Invitation to the Pilgrimage of Justice and Peace (Faith & Order Paper 224), 2019, ISBN: 978-2-8254-1725-6

Susan Durber and Fernando Enns (Eds.), *Walking Together: Reflections on the Ecumenical Pilgrimage of Justice and Peace,* Ebook edition, 2019, ISBN: 978-2-8254-1726-3

United and Uniting Churches: Two Messages (Faith & Order Paper 225), 2019, ISBN: 978-2-8254-1727-0

Pontifical Council for Interreligious Dialogue and the World Council of Churches, *Education for Peace in a Multi-Religious World: A Christian Perspective,* 2019, ISBN: 978-2-8254-1728-7

Moral Discernment in the Churches, Spanish edition, 2019, ISBN: 978-2-8254-1700-3

Moral Discernment in the Churches, German edition, 2019, ISBN: 978-2-8254-1729-4

Treatment Adherence and Faith Healing in the Context of HIV and AIDS in Africa (EHAIA), Kinwaranda Version, 2019, ISBN: 978-2-8254-1701-0

They Showed Us Unusual Kindness: Resources for the Week of Prayer for Christian Unity 2020 (Faith & Order Paper 226), 2019, ISBN: 978-2-8254-1704-1

Minutes of the Faith and Order Commission Meeting, (Nanjing, June 2019 (Faith & Order Paper 227), 2019, ISBN: 978-2-8254-1705-8

Fulata Lusungu Moyo, *Healing Together: A Facilitator's Resource for Ecumenical Faith and Community Community-Based Counselling* (EHAIA), 2019, ISBN: 978-2-8254-1706-5

Jürgen Moltmann, *Hope in These Troubled Times,* 2019, ISBN: 978-2-8254-1713-3

Mwai Mokoka, *Health-Promoting Churches: Reflections on Health and Healing for Churches on Commemorative World Health Days,* 2020, ISBN: 978-2-8254-1708-9

Mwai Mokoka, *Health-Promoting Churches: Reflections on Health and Healing for Churches on Commemorative World Health Days,* Spanish edition, 2020, ISBN: 978-2-8254-1709-6

Ecumenical International Youth Day, 2020: Young People and Mental Health, 2020, ISBN: 978-2-8254-1730-0

Climate Justice with and for Children and Youth in Churches: Get Informed, Get Inspired, Take Action, 2020, ISBN: 978-2-8254-1731-7

The Light of Peace: The Churches and the Korean Peninsula, 2020, ISBN: 978-2-8254-1732-4

Healing the World: Bible Studies for the Pandemic Era, 2020, ISBN: 978-2-8254-1733-1

The Light of Peace: Churches in Solidarity with the Korean Peninsula, 2020, ISBN: 978-2-8254-1734-8

Pontifical Council for Interreligious Dialogue and the World Council of Churches, *Serving a Wounded World in Interreligious Solidarity: A Christian call to reflection and action during COVID-19 and beyond,* 2020, ISBN: 978-2-8254-1737-9

Frederique Seidel and Emmanuel de Martel, *Cooler Earth — Higher Benefits: Actions by those who care about children, climate and finance,* 2020, ISBN: 978-2-8254-1748-5

Pilgrim Prayer: The Ecumenical Prayer Cycle, 2021, ISBN 978-2-8254-1666-2

Myriam Wiljens and Vladimir Shmaliy, eds., *Churches and Moral Discernment: Volume 1: Learning from Traditions,* (Faith & Order Paper 228), 2020, ISBN 978-2-8254-1735-5

Myriam Wijlens, Vladimir Shmaliy, and Simone Sinn, eds., *Churches and Moral Discernment: Volume 2: Learning from History,* (Faith & Order Paper 229), 2021, ISBN 978-2-8254-1736-2

Love and Witness: Proclaiming the Peace of the Lord Jesus Christ in a Religiously Plural World, (Faith & Order Paper 230), 2020, ISBN: 978-2-8254-1739-3

Cultivate and Care: An Ecumenical Theology of Justice for and within Creation, (Faith & Order Paper 226), 2020, ISBN: 978-2-8254-1738-6

Ellen Wondra, Stephanie Dietrich, and Ani Ghazaryan Drissi, eds., *Churches Respond To The Church: Towards A Common Vision, Volume I,* (Faith & Order Paper 231), 2021, ISBN: 978-2-8254-1750-8

Ellen Wondra, Stephanie Dietrich, and Ani Ghazaryan Drissi, eds., *Churches Respond To the Church: Towards a Common Vision, Volume II,* (Faith & Order Paper 232), 2021, ISBN: 978-2-8254-1751-5

Marianne Ejdersten et al., eds., *Voices of Lament, Hope, and Courage: A Week of Prayer in the Time of the COVID-19 Pandemic* (in 4 languages), 2021,
English: 978-2-8254-1757-7
French: 978-2-8254-1761-4
German: 978-2-8254-1759-1
Spanish: 978-2-8254-1760-7

Mwai Makoka, ed., *Health-Promoting Churches Volume II: A Handbook to Accompany Churches in Establishing and Running Sustainable Health Promotion Ministries,* 2021, ISBN: 978-2-8254-1754-6

Christ's Love Moves the World to Reconciliation and Unity: An introduction to the theme of the 11th Assembly of the World Council of Churches, Karlsruhe 2022 (in 9 languages), 2021/22,
English: 978-2-8254-1756-0
French: 978-2-8254-1798-0
German: 978-2-8254-1799-7
Spanish: 978-2-8254-1800-0
KiSwahili: 978-2-8254-1801-7
Portuguese: 978-2-8254-1802-4
Arabic: 978-2-8254-1803-1
Russian: 978-2-8254-1804-8
Indonesian: 978-2-8254-1805-5

Parce Que Dieu M'aime-Affirmer Ma Valeur En Christ: Un programme d'éducation chrétienne contra la violence basée sur le genre, 2021, ISBN: 978-2-8254-1753-9

Myriam Wijlens, Vladimir Shmaliy, and Simone Sinn, eds., *Churches and Moral Discernment Volume 3: Facilitating Dialogue to Build Koinonia,* 2021, ISBN: 978-2-8254-1762-1

Ellen Wondra, Stephanie Dietrich, and Ani Ghazaryan Drissi, eds., *What Are the Churches Saying About the Church? Key Findings and Proposals from the Responses to The Church: Towards a Common Vision,* (Faith & Order Paper 236), 2021, ISBN: 978-2-8254-1764-5

Darrell Jackson, Alessia Passarelli, eds., *Mapping Migration, Mapping Churches' Responses In Europe: Being Church Together,* Churches' Commission for Migrants in Europe, 2021, ISBN: 978-2-8254-1758-4

Peniel Jesudason Rufus Rajkumar, ed., *Faith(s) Seeking Justice: Liberation and the Rethinking of Interreligious Dialogue,* 2021, ISBN: 978-2-8254-1755-3

Churches' Commitments to Children, *Cooler Earth – Increased Benefits: Actions by Those who Care about Children, Climate and Finance (Second Edition),* 2021, ISBN: 978-2-8254-1763-8

Ecumenical International Youth Day Event Toolkit 2021: Young People and Climate Change, 2021, ISBN: 978-2-8254-1772-0

Walk the Talk: A Toolkit to Accompany the "Roadmap for Congregations, Communities and Churches for an Economy of Life and Ecological Justice," 2021, ISBN: 978-2-8254-1773-7

Petter Jakobsson, Risto Jukko, and Olle Kristenson, eds., *Sharing and Learning: Bible, Mission, and Receptive Ecumenism,* 2021, ISBN: 978-2-8254-1766-9

Thursdays in Black Bible Studies Series 1: Listening, Learning and Responding to the Word of God, 2021, ISBN: 978-2-8254-1779-9

Risto Jukko, ed., *Call to Discipleship: Mission in the Pilgrimage of Justice and Peace,* 2021, ISBN: 978-2-8254-1773-7

New International Financial and Economic Architecture initiative (NIFEA), *ZacTax Toolkit,* 2021, ISBN: 978-3-949281-03-7

Jennifer Philpot-Nissen, *Killer Robots: A Campaign Guide for Churches,* 2021, ISBN: 978-2-8254-1775-1

Jennifer Philpot-Nissen, *Les Robots tueurs: Guide de campagne pour les Églises,* 2021, ISBN: 978-2-8254-1783-6

Jennifer Philpot-Nissen, *Killer-Roboter: Ein Kampagnen-Leitfaden für Kirchen,* 2021, 978-2-8254-1784-3

Jennifer Philpot-Nissen, *Robots asesinos: Guía de campaña para las Iglesias,* 2021, ISBN: 978-2-8254-1785-0

Jennifer Philpot-Nissen, *Arabic edition, Killer Robots,* 2021. ISBN: 978-2-8254-1786-7

Jennifer Philpot-Nissen, *Robôs Assassinos: Um Guia de Campanha para as Igrejas,* 2021, ISBN: 978-2-8254-1787-4

Isabel Apawo Phiri, Collins Shava, eds., *The Africa We Pray For on a Pilgrimage of Justice and Peace: PJP Series Vol 1,* 2021, Web ISBN 978-2-88931-417-1, Print ISBN 978-2-88931-371-6

Joy Eva Bohol, Benjamin Simon, eds., *Let the Waves Roar: Perspectives of Young Prophetic Voices in the Ecumenical Movement,* 2021, ISBN: 978-2-8254-1765-2

Louk A. Andrianos, Tom Sverre Tomren, eds., *Contemporary Ecotheology, Climate Justice and Environmental Stewardship in World Religions: Ecothee Volume 6 - Orthodox Academy of Crete.* Published by Embla Akademis, 2021, ISBN: 978-82-93689-14-0

Ellen Wondra, Stephanie Dietrich, Ani Ghazaryan Drissi, eds., *Common Threads: Key Themes from Responses to The Church: Towards a Common Vision,* Faith and Order Paper No 233, 2021, ISBN: 978-2-8254-1776-8

Pilgrims on the Path of Peace. The Journey of the WCC from Busan to Karlsruhe. (Unillustrated), 2022, ISBN: 978-2-8254-1789-8

Pilgerinnen und Pilger auf dem Weg des Friedens. Die Reise des ÖRK von Busan nach Karlsruhe (ohne Bilder), 2022 ISBN: 978-2-8254-1792-8

Peregrinos en el camino de la paz. El recorrido del CMI de Busan a Karlsruhe (sin ilustraciones), 2022, ISBN: 978-2-8254-1791-1

Pèlerins sur la route de la paix. Le Cheminement du COE de Busan à Karlsruhe (non illustré), 2022, ISBN: 978-2-8254-1790-4

Archbishop Dr Anastasios, *Coexistence: Peace, Nature, Poverty, Terrorism, Values (Religious Perspectives),* translated by John Chryssavgis. 2021, ISBN: 978-2-8254-1752-2

Semegnish Asfaw, ed., *I Belong, Volume 2: Biblical Reflections on Statelessness,* 2022, ISBN: 978-2-8254-1780-5

Celebrate Christ's Love! Sing and Pray, 2022, ISBN: 978-2-8254-1788-1

Fernando Enns, Upolu Lumā Vaai, Andrés Pacheco Lozano, and Betty Pries, eds., *Transformative Spiritualities for the Pilgrimage of Justice and Peace:* PJP Series Vol 2, 2022, ISBN: 978-2-88931-458-4.

Called to Transformation - Ecumenical Diakonia, ISBN: 978-2-8254-1806-2.

Her-Stories of Transformation, Justice, and Peace: Report on the Women of Faith Pilgrimages, 2022, ISBN: 978-2-8254-1811-6.

Kuzipa Nalwamba Maritta Ruhland, eds., *GETI 2022: Christ's Love (Re)Moves Borders: An Ecumenical Reader,* 2022, ISBN: 978-2-8254-1807-9

Globethics.net Publications

The list below is only a selection of our publications. To view the full collection, please visit our website.

All free products are provided free of charge and can be downloaded in PDF form from the Globethics.net library and at www.globethics.net/publications. Bulk print copies can be ordered from publications@globethics.net at special rates from the Global South.

Paid products not provided free of charge are indicated*.

The Director of the different Series of Globethics.net Publications:

Prof. Dr. Obiora Ike, Executive Director of Globethics.net in Geneva and Professor of Ethics at the Godfrey Okoye University Enugu/Nigeria.

Contact for manuscripts and suggestions: publications@globethics.net

Global Series

Christoph Stückelberger, Walter Fust, Obiora Ike (eds.), *Global Ethics for Leadership. Values and Virtues for Life*, 2016, 444pp. ISBN: 978–2–88931–123–1

Dietrich Werner / Elisabeth Jeglitzka (eds.), *Eco-Theology, Climate Justice and Food Security: Theological Education and Christian Leadership Development*, 316pp. 2016, ISBN 978–2–88931–145–3

Obiora Ike, Andrea Grieder and Ignace Haaz (eds.), *Poetry and Ethics: Inventing Possibilities in Which We Are Moved to Action and How We Live Together,* 271pp. 2018, ISBN 978–2–88931–242–9

Christoph Stückelberger and Pavan Duggal (eds.), *Cyber Ethics 4.0: Serving Humanity with Values,* 503pp. 2018, ISBN 978–2–88931–264-1

Texts Series

Ethics in the Information Society: The Nine 'P's. A Discussion Paper for the WSIS+10 Process 2013–2015, 2013, 32pp. ISBN: 978–2–940428–063–2

Principles on Equality and Inequality for a Sustainable Economy. Endorsed by the Global Ethics Forum 2014 with Results from Ben Africa Conference 2014, 2015, 41pp. ISBN: 978–2–88931–025–8

Water Ethics: Principles and Guidelines, 2019, 41pp. ISBN 978–2–88931-313-6, available in four languages.

Theses Series

Sabina Kavutha Mutisya, *The Experience of Being a Divorced or Separated Single Mother: A Phenomenological Study,* 2019, 168pp. ISBN: 978-2-88931-274-0

Florence Muia, *Sustainable Peacebuilding Strategies. Sustainable Peacebuilding Operations in Nakuru County, Kenya: Contribution to the Catholic Justice and Peace Commission (CJPC),* 2020, 195pp. ISBN: 978-2-88931-331-0

Mary Rose-Claret Ogbuehi, *The Struggle for Women Empowerment Through Education,* 2020, 410pp. ISBN: 978-2-88931-363-1

Paul K. Musolo W'Isuka, Missional *Encounter: Approach for Ministering to Invisible Peoples,* 2021, 462pp. ISBN: 978-2-88931-401-0

Andrew Danjuma Dewan, *Media Ethics and the Case of Ethnicity A Contextual Analysis in Plateau State, Nigeria,* 2022, 369pp. ISBN 978-2-88931-436-2

Focus Series

Maryann Ijeoma Egbujor, *The Relevance of Journalism Education in Kenya for Professional Identity and Ethical Standards,* 2018, 141pp. ISBN: 978–2–88931233–7

Christoph, Stückelberger, *Globalance. Ethics Handbook for a Balanced World Post-Covid,* 2020, 608pp. ISBN: 978-2-88931-368-6

Bosco Muchukiwa Rukakiza, *Résilience et transformation des conflits dans les États des Grands Lacs africains: Théorie, démarches et applications,* 2021, 126pp. ISBN 978-2-88931-405-8

Praxis Series

Benoît Girardin / Evelyne Fiechter-Widemann (eds.), *Éthique de l'eau: Pour un usage et une gestion justes et durables des ressources en eau,* 2020, 309pp. ISBN: 978-2-88931-337-2

Didier Ostermann, *Le rôle de l'Église maronite dans la construction du Liban:1500 ans d'histoire, du Ve au XXe siècle,* 2020, 142pp. ISBN: 978-2-88931-365-5

Elli Kansiime, *Theology of Work and Development,* 2020, 158pp. ISBN: 978-2-88931-373-0

Christoph Stückelberger (ed.), *Corruption-free Religions are Possible: Integrity, Stewardship, Accountability*, 2021, 295pp. ISBN: 978-2-88931-422-5

André Masiala ma Solo, *Les enfants de personne : étude clinique et de phénoménologie sociale sur l'enfance défavorisée en RD Congo*, 2022, 158pp. ISBN 978-2-88931-420-1

African Law Series

Pascal Mukonde Musulay, *Démocratie électorale en Afrique subsaharienne: Entre droit, pouvoir et argent*, 2016, 209pp. ISBN 978–2–88931–156–9

Pascal Mukonde Musulay, *Droits, libertés et devoirs de la personne et des peuples en droit international africain Tome I Promotion et protection*, 282pp. 2021, ISBN 978-2-88931-397-6

Pascal Mukonde Musulay, *Droits, libertés et devoirs de la personne et des peuples en droit international africain Tome II Libertés, droits et obligations démocratiques*, 332pp. 2021, ISBN 978-2-88931-399-0

Ambroise Katambu Bulambo, *Règlement judiciaire des conflits électoraux. Précis de droit comparé africain*, 2021, 672pp., ISBN 978-2-88931-403-4

Osita C. Eze, *Africa Charter on Rights & Duties, Enforcement Mechanism*, 2021, 406pp, ISBN 978-2-88931-414-0

Agape Series

崔万田 Cui Wantian, *爱+经济学 Agape Economics*, 2020, 420pp. ISBN: 978-2-88931-349-5

Cui Wantian, Christoph Stückelberger, *The Better Sinner: A Practical Guide on Corruption, 2020*, 37pp. ISBN: 978-2-88931-339-6 (Available also in Chinese).

Anh Tho Andres Kammler, *FaithInvest: Impactful Cooperation. Report of the International Conference Geneva 2020*, 2020, 70pp. ISBN: 978-2-88931-357-0

崔万田Cui Wantian, 价值观创造价值　　企业家信仰于企业绩效 *Values Create Value. Impact through Faith-based Entrepreneurship*, 2020, 432pp. IBSN: 978-2-88931-361-7

Moses C. 编辑, 圣商灵粮：中国基督徒企业家的灵修日记*Daily Bread for Christians in Business: The Spiritual Diary of Chinese Christian Entrepreneurs*, 412pp. 2021, ISBN 978-2-88931-391-4

Haicun Kong, *Walk the Talk. Africa / Asia Focus. Report of the International Online Conference, Jan / Mar 2021*, 2021, 41pp. ISBN 978-2-88931- 411-9

China Christian Series

Spirituality 4.0 at the Workplace and FaithInvest - Building Bridges, 2019, 107pp. ISBN: 978-2-88931-304-4

海茵兹·吕格尔 / 克里斯多夫·芝格里斯特 (Christoph Sigrist/ Heinz Rüegger) *Diaconia: An Introduction. Theological Foundation of Christian Service*, 2019, 433pp. ISBN: 978-2-88931-302-0

Vietnam Ethics Series

Anh Tho Andres (ed.), *Vietnam in Transition: Education, Culture and Ethics. A Reader and Curriculum, Vietnam Hoc English Edition, 2022*, 255pp. ISBN 978-2-88931-450-8

Education Ethics Series

Divya Singh / Christoph Stückelberger (eds.), *Ethics in Higher Education Values-driven Leaders for the Future*, 2017, 367pp. ISBN: 978–2–88931–165–1

Obiora Ike / Chidiebere Onyia (eds.), *Ethics in Higher Education, Foundation for Sustainable Development*, 2018, 645pp. ISBN: 978-2-88931-217-7

Obiora Ike / Chidiebere Onyia (eds.), *Ethics in Higher Education, Religions and Traditions in Nigeria* 2018, 198pp. ISBN: 978-2-88931-219-1

Obiora F. Ike, Justus Mbae, Chidiebere Onyia (eds.), *Mainstreaming Ethics in Higher Education: Research Ethics in Administration, Finance, Education, Environment and Law Vol. 1*, 2019, 779pp. ISBN 978-2-88931-300-6

Ikechukwu J. Ani/Obiora F. Ike (eds.), *Higher Education in Crisis Sustaining Quality Assurance and Innovation in Research through Applied Ethics*, 2019, 214pp. ISBN 978-2-88931-323-5

Deivit Montealegre / María Eugenia Barroso (eds.), *Ethics in Higher Education, a Transversal Dimension: Challenges for Latin America. Ética en educación superior, una dimensión transversal: Desafíos para América Latina*, 2020, 148pp. ISBN 978-2-88931-359-4

Obiora Ike, Justus Mbae, Chidiebere Onyia, Herbert Makinda (eds.), *Mainstreaming Ethics in Higher Education Vol. 2*, 2021, 420pp. ISBN: 978-2-88931-383-9

Christoph Stückelberger/ Joseph Galgalo/ Samuel Kobia (eds.), *Leadership with Integrity. Higher Education from Vocation to Funding*, 2021, 288pp. ISBN 978-2-88931-389-1

Jacinta M. Adhiambo and Florentina N. Ndeke (eds.), *Educating Teachers for Tomorrow: on Ethics and quality in Pedagogical Formation*, 2021, 196pp. ISBN: 978-2-88931-407-2

Erin Green / Divya Singh / Roland Chia (eds.), *AI Ethics and Higher Education Good Practice and Guidance for Educators, Learners, and Institutions*, 2022, 324pp. ISBN 978-2-88931-442-3

Copublications & Other

Obiora F. Ike, *Moral and Ethical Leadership, Human Rights and Conflict Resolution – African and Global Contexts*, 2020, 191pp. ISBN: 978-2-88931-333-4

Kenneth R. Ross, *Mission Rediscovered: Transforming Disciples*, 2020, 138pp. ISBN 978-2-88931-369-3

Obiora Ike, Amélé Adamavi-Aho Ekué, Anja Andriamay, Lucy Howe López (eds.), *Who Cares About Ethics?* 2020, 352pp. ISBN 978-2-88931-381-5

Fanny Iona Morel, *Whispers from the Land of Snows: Culture-based Violence in Tibet.* 2021, 218pp. ISBN: 978-2-88931-418-8

Ignace Haaz / Amélé Adamavi-Aho Ekué (eds.), *Walking with the Earth. Intercultural Perspectives on Ethics of Ecological Caring*, 2022, 324pp. ISBN 978-2-88931-434-8

Christoph Stückelberger, *My Cross – My Life: Daily Spiritual Joy*, 2022, 137pp. ISBN 978-2-88931-446-1

Abdeljalil Akkari, Stefania Gandolfi, Moussa Mohamed Sagayar (eds.), *Repenser l'éducation et la pédagogie dans une perspective africaine Manuel pratique à destination des enseignants et des formateurs d'enseignants*, 2022, 220pp. ISBN 978-2-88931-454-6

This is only a selection of our latest publications, to view our full collection please visit:

www.globethics.net/publications

9 782889 314751